PAULA
MODERSOHN-
BECKER
MUSEUM

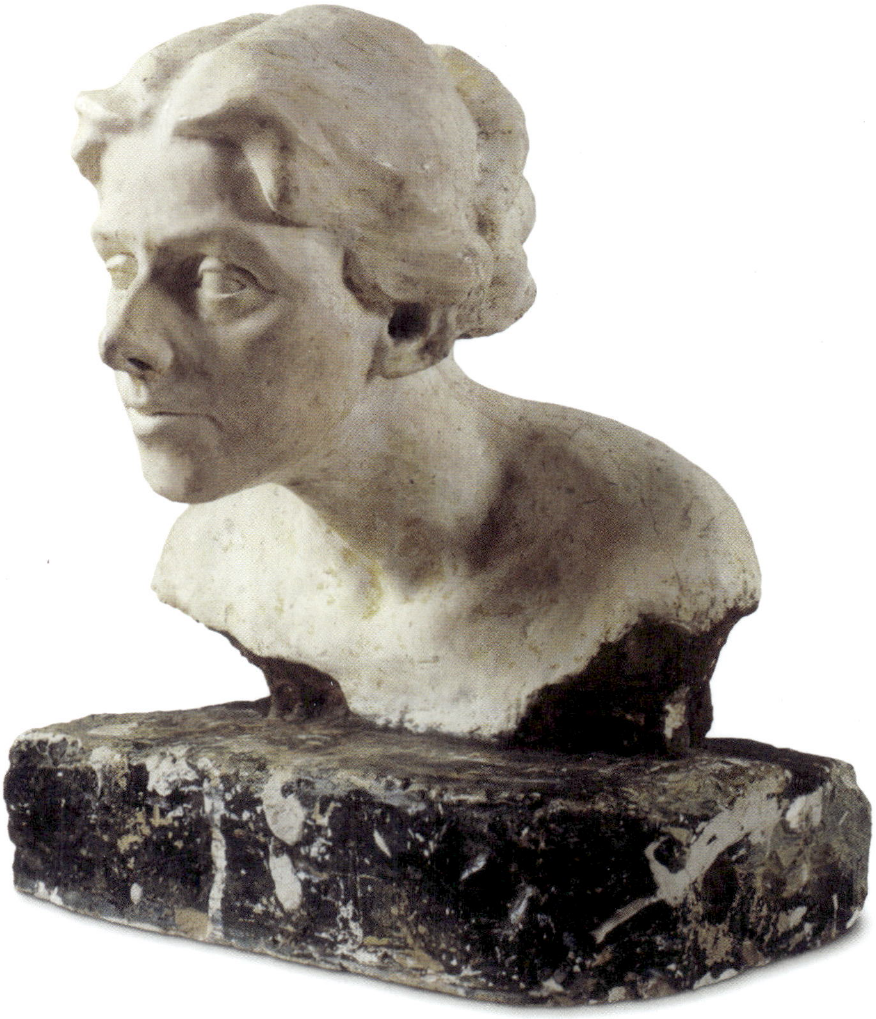

Clara Rilke-Westhoff
Portrait of the Painter Paula Modersohn-Becker, 1899

A publication by the
Paula Modersohn-Becker Museum
on the occasion of the exhibition
Becoming Paula. London Berlin Worpswede Paris
Edited by Frank Schmidt

Bremen, 2026

PAULA

LONDON
BERLIN
WORPSWEDE
PARIS

MODERSOHN-BECKER

HIRMER

BECOMING PAULA. BRACINGLY MODERN

FRANK SCHMIDT

It was a relatively short creative period. Paula Modersohn-Becker had only around ten years in which to create a respectable body of work comprising almost 750 paintings and more than 1,400 drawings. But she did not know that the time available to her would be so short.

The exhibition *Becoming Paula* takes us on a journey through time, from 1892 to 1907, guided along the way by some of her most enigmatic and moving paintings and drawings. Developments and continuities become visible, as do references to traditions and courageous steps into a new era. *The New York Times* hails her as a groundbreaking artist, describing her work as "bracingly modern".[1] In 2024, two exhibitions in New York and Chicago introduced the German painter to the American public for the first time. She is well known in Germany. However, the American reviewer's unadulterated view makes us aware of how unusual, bold and novel her work must have seemed to first-time viewers here as well. To this day, it is astonishing how the young painter was able to create a painting such as *Brustbild eines Mädchens in der Sonne vor weiter Landschaft* (Bust Portrait of a Girl in the Sun in front of a Wide Landscape; fig. p. 30) as early as 1897. What makes this painting spectacular is not its motif but rather its composition, namely the boldness with which the figure is placed in front of this landscape with an extremely high horizon line. The figure and the landscape do not appear homogeneous, and yet they are directly connected, not least by the horizon cutting through the girl's head.

Her extensive oeuvre of drawings remained virtually unknown for a long time, even to many of her admirers. In her fascinating pastel drawings, Paula Modersohn-Becker

1 Arthur Lubow, "Illuminating a Trailblazing Artist Who Died Too Young", *The New York Times*, 14 August 2024 (updated 19 August 2024), https://www.nytimes.com/2024/08/14/arts/design/paula-modersohn-becker-art-neue-galerie-review.html [accessed 11 December 2025].

captures the essence of her subjects without pathos or social criticism. A prime example of this is *Alte blinde sitzende Frau* (Seated Old Blind Woman, 1898/99; fig. p. 19). The artist is close to her model yet remains detached. She does not involve herself, and it is precisely for this reason that she manages to portray her subjects so truthfully and authentically that they still speak to us today.

The young Paula Becker was also capable of creating large-scale works. Her charcoal drawing *Stehender männlicher Akt nach links* (Standing Male Nude Facing Left, 1898; fig. p. 73) is particularly impressive. Such life-size, full-body nudes on paper are extremely rare, and few have survived due to the delicate nature of the material. Moreover, drawing the entire figure in life-size format was not common academic practice. It was the artist Fritz Mackensen, under whose supervision she worked in Worpswede in 1898–99, who instructed her in this exercise in drawing a naturalistically conceived man. Even at this early stage of her development, her desire to achieve greater formal coherence in her depictions of the human body is evident.

As one of the most important subjects in art history, the nude played an increasingly central role in her work, evident not only in her countless nude studies, but also in her paintings. Her *Selbstbildnis am 6. Hochzeitstag* (Self-Portrait on the 6th Wedding Anniversary, 1906; fig. p. 83) and *Liegende Mutter mit Kind II* (Reclining Mother with Child II, 1906; fig. pp. 70/71) are much-described icons within her oeuvre. It is still remarkable today how matter-of-factly Modersohn-Becker was the first to depict an unclothed mother with her child in painting: unembellished and immediate. The inherent bond between mother and child is captured here in a unique way. No less "singular" is *Sitzender Mädchenakt mit angezogenen Beinen I* (Seated Girl Nude with Her Legs Drawn Up I, c. 1904; fig. p. 79). The barely differentiated background makes the girl huddled on the floor – her stepdaughter, Elsbeth, according to Otto Modersohn – appear all the more pictorially powerful. This contrasts with the figure's closed posture centred purely on herself. When had children ever been depicted as being so vulnerable while also revealing their state of mind to the onlooker?

The approximately one hundred self-portraits, comprising paintings, drawings, watercolours and pastels, constitute a world unto themselves. From her early works on paper to her later paintings, a transformation takes place which, with a few exceptions, is accompanied by a departure from naturalistic representation. In a letter to the collector Karl Ernst Osthaus in Hagen in March 1913, Paula's mother expressed the following assessment: "I find all of Paula's self-portraits cruel to her sweetness. How can one treat beauty so harshly!" His reply is also revealing. He had met the painter in person and, in 1913, acquired *Selbstbildnis mit Kamelienzweig* (Self-Portrait with Sprig of Camellias, 1906/07; fig. p. 54) for the Museum Folkwang in Hagen: "I do find a great similarity in it, and strangely enough, it is precisely the impression that I myself have of your daughter. I would not even have recognised her from the other pictures."[2] Ottilie Reylaender, a painter friend from Worpswede, judged: "No picture, no photograph, not even a self-portrait, fully captures her."[3] The magnificent *Selbstbildnis mit Zitrone* (Self-Portrait with Lemon, 1906/07; fig. p. 55) confirms the observations of both Osthaus and Reylaender. While the young Paula Becker portrayed herself in her studio as self-confident and easily recognisable during her first stay in Paris in 1900 (fig. p. 21), she appears strangely distant in the 1906/07 painting. She had previously studied Egyptian mummy portraits in the Louvre and was fascinated by their simplicity and expressiveness. She wanted to recreate this very expression in her own portraits, irrespective of the intended resemblance to the deceased in the ancient images. She also went beyond these in formal terms. Colour-accentuated outlines hold the forms together. The austerity of the composition is broken up by free painting with strong

[2] Correspondence between Mathilde Becker and Karl Ernst Osthaus, 6 March 1913; Karl Ernst Osthaus Archive, Hagen, F2/1364/1–2; quoted in Frank Schmidt, "Vorwort und Dank", in *Ich bin Ich. Paula Modersohn-Becker. Die Selbstbildnisse*, ed. Frank Schmidt, exh. cat. Paula Modersohn-Becker Museum, Bremen (Munich 2019), pp. 9–11, here p. 11 [translated].

[3] Rolf Hetsch (ed.), *Paula Modersohn-Becker. Ein Buch der Freundschaft* [*Die Zeichner des Volkes*, vol. 4], (Berlin 1932), p. 38 [translated].

colour contrasts. This is no longer a self-portrait – but a painting that stands up to comparison with contemporary works by Pablo Picasso and Henri Matisse.

From 1905 on, Paul Modersohn-Becker turned her attention to another major subject in art history, creating a series of impressive still lifes that are striking in their colourfulness and rich painting style. Examples include *Stillleben mit Milchsatte* (Still Life with Milk Bowl, 1905; fig. p. 63) and *Stillleben mit Kürbis und Ingwertopf* (Still Life with Pumpkin and Ginger Pot, c. 1905; fig. p. 62). This is magnificent and mature *peinture*, which no longer seeks to be anything more than that, without allegorical or symbolic iconography. Colour, composition and painting – *c'est tout*.

There is much talk, writing and, not infrequently, speculation about how Modersohn-Becker's work was perceived by friends, relatives and fellow artists. As is often the case in marriages between artists, the Modersohns showed each other their new paintings and discussed them. With the German sculptor Bernhard Hoetger, whom she visited in Paris in 1906 and with whom she quickly became friends, there was a lively exchange about art, including his and hers. Years later, he still had vivid memories of his first visit to her studio: "There, I experienced a miracle, quietly and deeply moved. [...] I could only tell her: 'They are all great works.'"[4] Shortly afterwards, she wrote to him: "That you believe in me is the most beautiful belief in the whole world, because I believe in you. [...] You have given me myself. Now I have courage. [...] Now I have begun to believe that I shall become somebody."[5] Hoetger was a source of encouragement to her during a personally difficult and decisive phase of her development, in which she sometimes doubted herself. But how did she herself view her work? Occasional brief hints appear in her letters and diary entries, but these mostly describe to her correspondents what she has painted or speak in general terms of her desire to create good, lasting works. A casual sketch of her Paris studio, preserved on an envelope (fig. p. 90), is more revealing. The three identifiable paintings on the wall seem to have been important to her. From left to right, they are *Lee Hoetger vor Blumengrund* (Lee Hoetger in front of a Floral Background; fig. p. 51), *Frau mit Katze und Papagei* (Woman with Cat and Parrot; war loss 1943) and *Liegende Mutter mit Kind II* (fig. pp. 70/71), all from her then current production in 1906. Through these paintings, Modersohn-Becker becomes aware of what she has already achieved and where her path will lead her. Her assessment was not mistaken. The two outer works are among her major works, which are requested for every retrospective, and the middle one would undoubtedly also play in this league. In addition to the undeniable influence of Paul Gauguin, there are also astounding parallels with Picasso on the eve of Cubism – although Modersohn-Becker would not have been aware of his corresponding works. In this painting, she combines the archaic with the modern and introduces an exotic touch, accentuated by colour, that had not previously been present in her work.[6] Unlike her previous nudes, which depicted herself, children or mothers with children, the animals and still life in the foreground remove the naked woman from any Worpswede or even Parisian context. The composition seems contrived, unlike Gauguin's South Sea paintings, for example. Modersohn-Becker also does not depict figures in landscapes that she has not visited herself. This fundamentally contradicts her claim to authenticity and the truth of art.

One visitor to the studio was Rainer Maria Rilke, who had been able to follow her work every once in a while from 1900 on. In 1906, he became aware of the novel and revolutionary nature of her painting: "The strange thing was finding Modersohn's wife busy with her very own development in painting, working heedless of all else and with such determination, on things that [...] could not have been seen or painted there before by anyone. And she has this approach that is very much her own, strangely akin to van Gogh and his style."[7]

[4] Bernhard Hoetger, "Erinnerungen an Paula Modersohn", in Carl Emil Uphoff, *Paula Modersohn* [*Junge Kunst*, vol. 2], (Leipzig 1919), unpaginated [translated].

[5] Letter from Paula Modersohn-Becker to Bernhard Hoetger, Paris, 5 May 1906, in *Paula Modersohn-Becker. The Letters and Journals*, ed. Günter Busch and Liselotte von Reinken, revised and expanded edition, ed. and trans. Arthur S. Wensinger and Carole Clew Hoey (New York 1983), p. 393.

[6] In the 1913 catalogue raisonné compiled by Curt Stoermer, the face is described as "lila-violett" (purple-violet).

Apart from Rainer Maria Rilke, Otto Modersohn, Bernhard Hoetger and her sister Herma, only a few people were able to see these and the more than 700 other paintings and countless drawings in the Paris or Worpswede studio during her lifetime. But this oeuvre did not remain without consequences. Just a few years after Modersohn-Becker's death, a selection of her letters and diaries was published, and her works were exhibited and acquired by important collectors. Since then, numerous artists have engaged with her work, whether as a homage, as in the work of Georg Baselitz, Marikke Heinz-Hoek and Chantal Joffe; as a model, as in the work of Gudrun Brüne; or as a copy, as in the work of Fritz Winter, who was just starting his career. None of these artists is an imitator or "follower", as we would say today. They saw something in this work and this artist that gave them cause for reflection. In a 2013 interview, Georg Baselitz stated: "Modersohn-Becker's paintings are undoubtedly among the best paintings produced in Germany since the turn of the twentieth century."[8]

A solitary work such as that of Paula Modersohn-Becker is bound to provoke contradictory responses and criticism. Richard Hamann, for example, passed harsh judgement in 1925. He claimed that she took no risks in her painting and that one had to "always read letters and diary entries aloud in order to fully comprehend what is presented as pure art".[9] However, given that she painted the first female self-portrait in art history (fig. p. 83) and had such a demanding attitude towards herself and others, it is difficult to argue that she lacked daring when she remained uncompromisingly true to her own path. It is also a misunderstanding when Hamann demands, as it were, a literary accompaniment to the images that he finds seemingly meaningless. The clarity of her work lies precisely in her ability to strip away everything that is vague and uncertain, and to approach the condensed essence of the motif, detached from anything anecdotal.

In the exhibition *Becoming Paula*, external and internal perspectives intertwine, and the images are overlaid with the many views of her work to date. Numerous monographs, books and texts, and more recently films, paint many pictures of Paula Modersohn-Becker, who primarily speaks to us through her works. In all these attempts at approximation, including in this essay, it is inevitable that the authors' perspectives will influence the narrative and that Modersohn-Becker will become a projection screen – for instance, as an example of women artists unseen during their lifetime, of emancipation or feminism. Clichés persist, such as the thoroughly refuted claim that Otto Modersohn did not understand or support his wife's work,[10] or that she was isolated as an artist. She did not see herself as a feminist either. Given her upper-class background and upbringing, this would hardly have been compatible. She simply wanted to do what she saw as her calling: to paint. The fact that she did this in a predominantly male-dominated art world was a hindrance – but ultimately did not prevent her from following her path.

Is it therefore possible to fully understand Paula Modersohn-Becker as a person and painter? This exhibition, too, will and must fail in this endeavour. During her lifetime, her relatives and friends had their own perception of her. But even they were hardly able to get close to her. The words of her sister and confidante Herma probably sum it up best: "She loved her solitude and undisturbed life. And her mystery, which always surrounded her somehow."[11]

7 Letter from Rainer Maria Rilke to Karl von der Heydt, Meudon, 16 January 1906, quoted in https://www.pmb-stiftung.de/E_biographie.html [accessed 12 December 2025].

8 Georg Baselitz in an interview conducted by Hartwig Fischer, in *Georg Baselitz. Hintergrundgeschichten*, exh. cat. Staatliche Kunstsammlungen Dresden (Munich 2013), p. 54 [translated].

9 Richard Hamann, *Die deutsche Malerei vom Rokoko bis zum Expressionismus* (Leipzig/Berlin 1925), pp. 465–66 [translated].

10 See, among others, *Paula Modersohn-Becker. Otto Modersohn. Der Briefwechsel*, ed. Antje Modersohn and Wolfgang Werner (Berlin 2017).

11 Quoted in Hetsch 1932 (see note 3), p. 17 [translated].

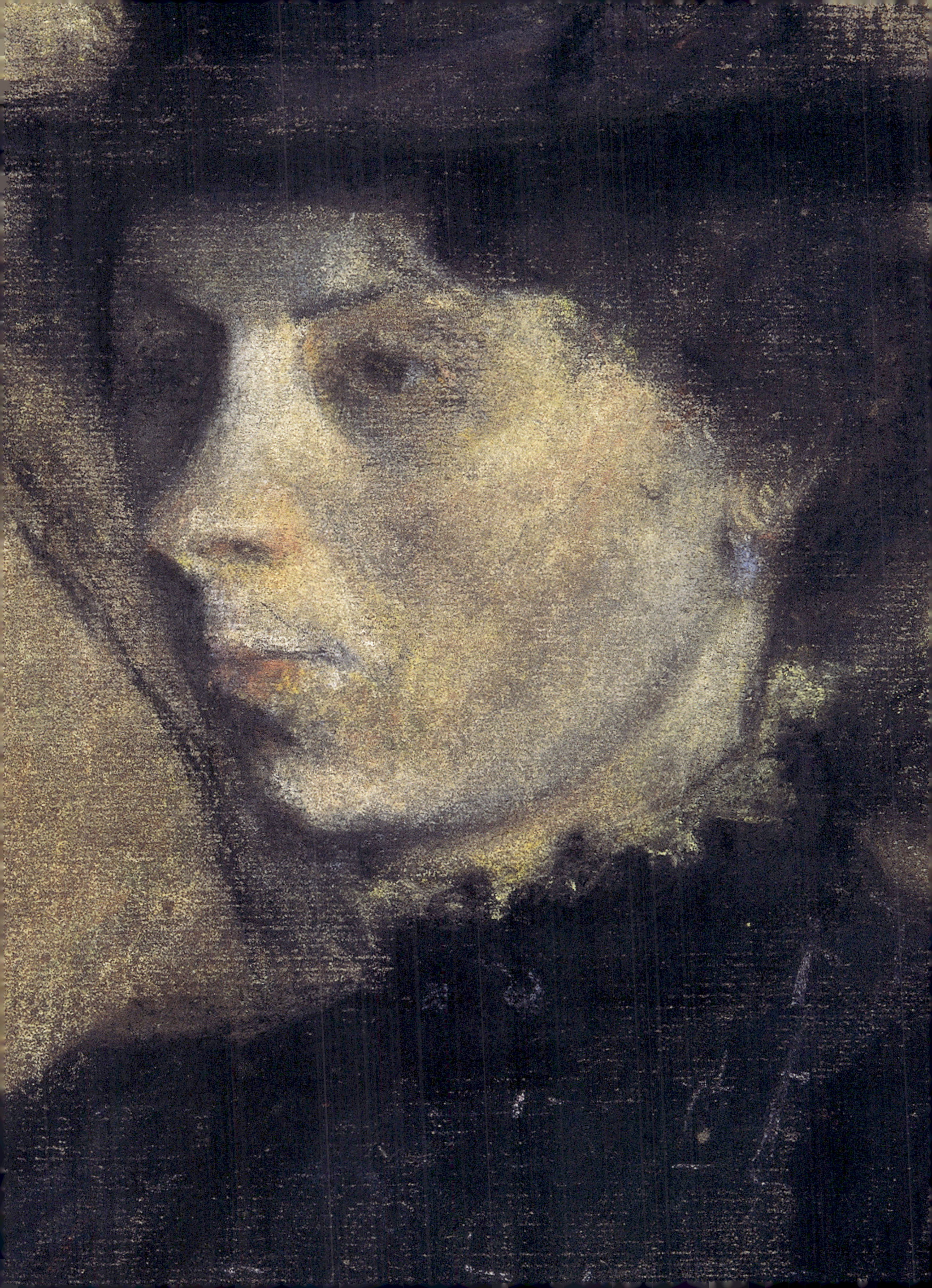

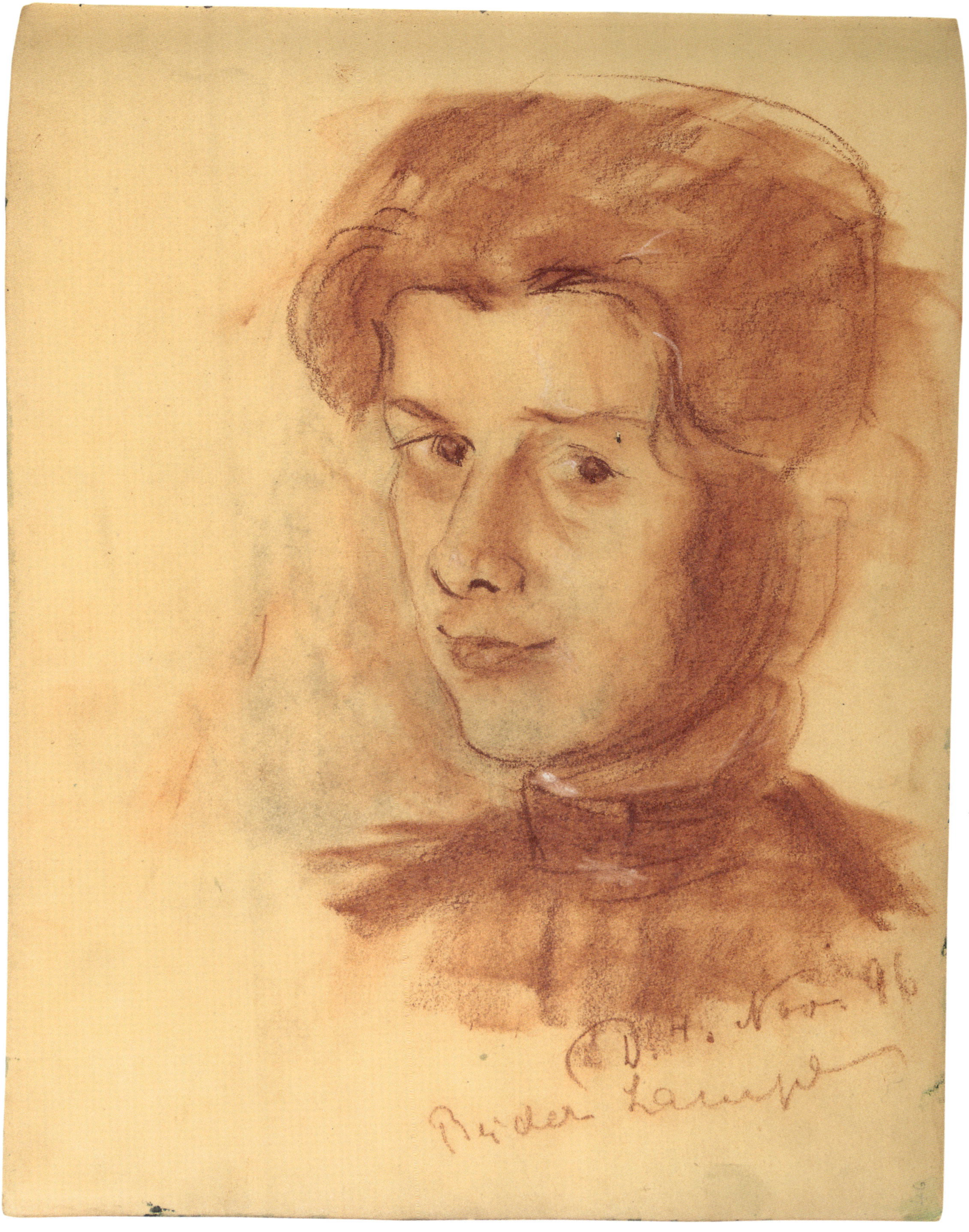

Self-Portrait by Lamplight, 1896

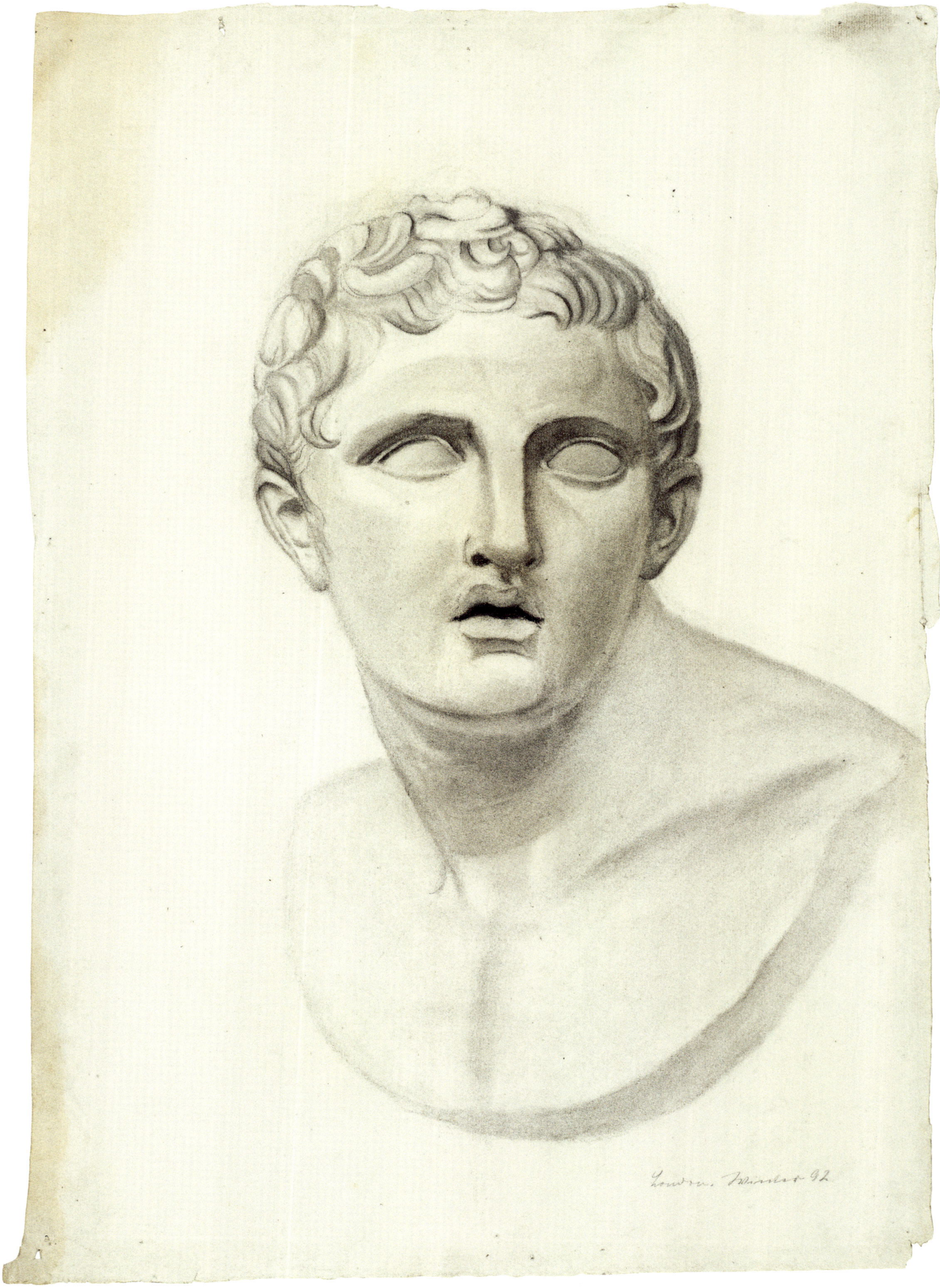

Drawing Based on a Bust of a Greek Youth with His Mouth Open, 1892

Goblet and Cylinder, 1891

3

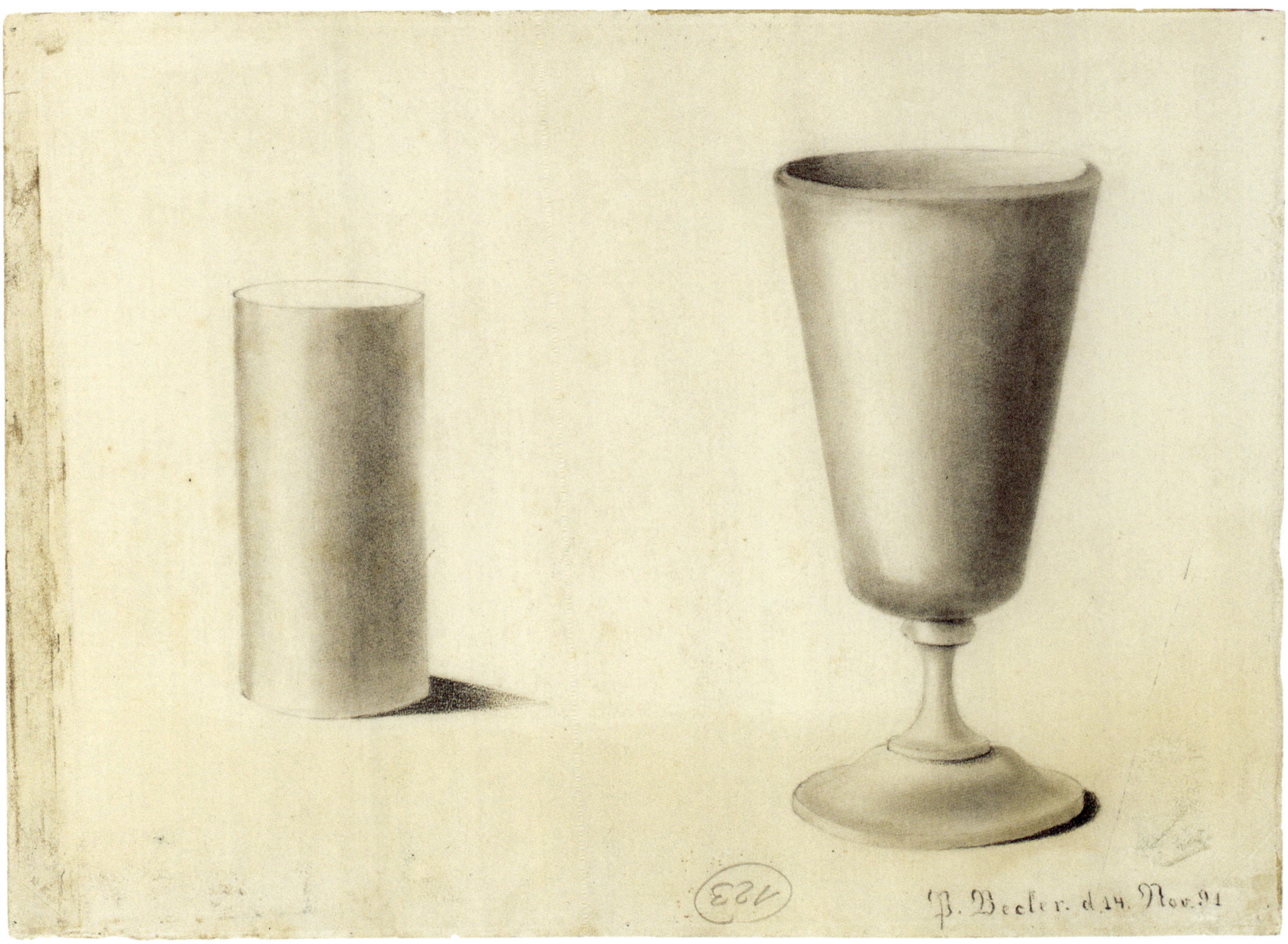

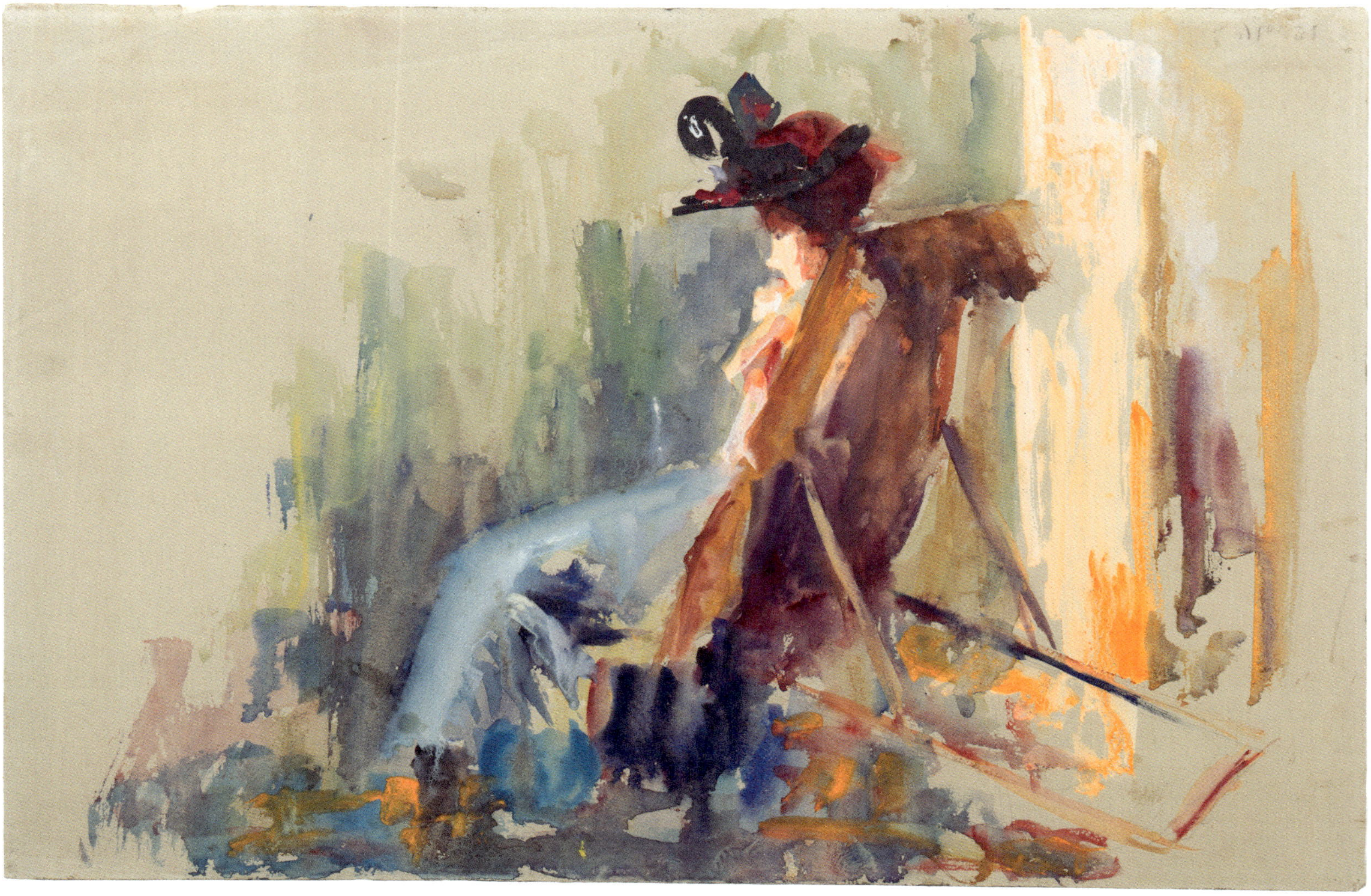

Lady with Hat in a Deckchair, Berlin 1896/97

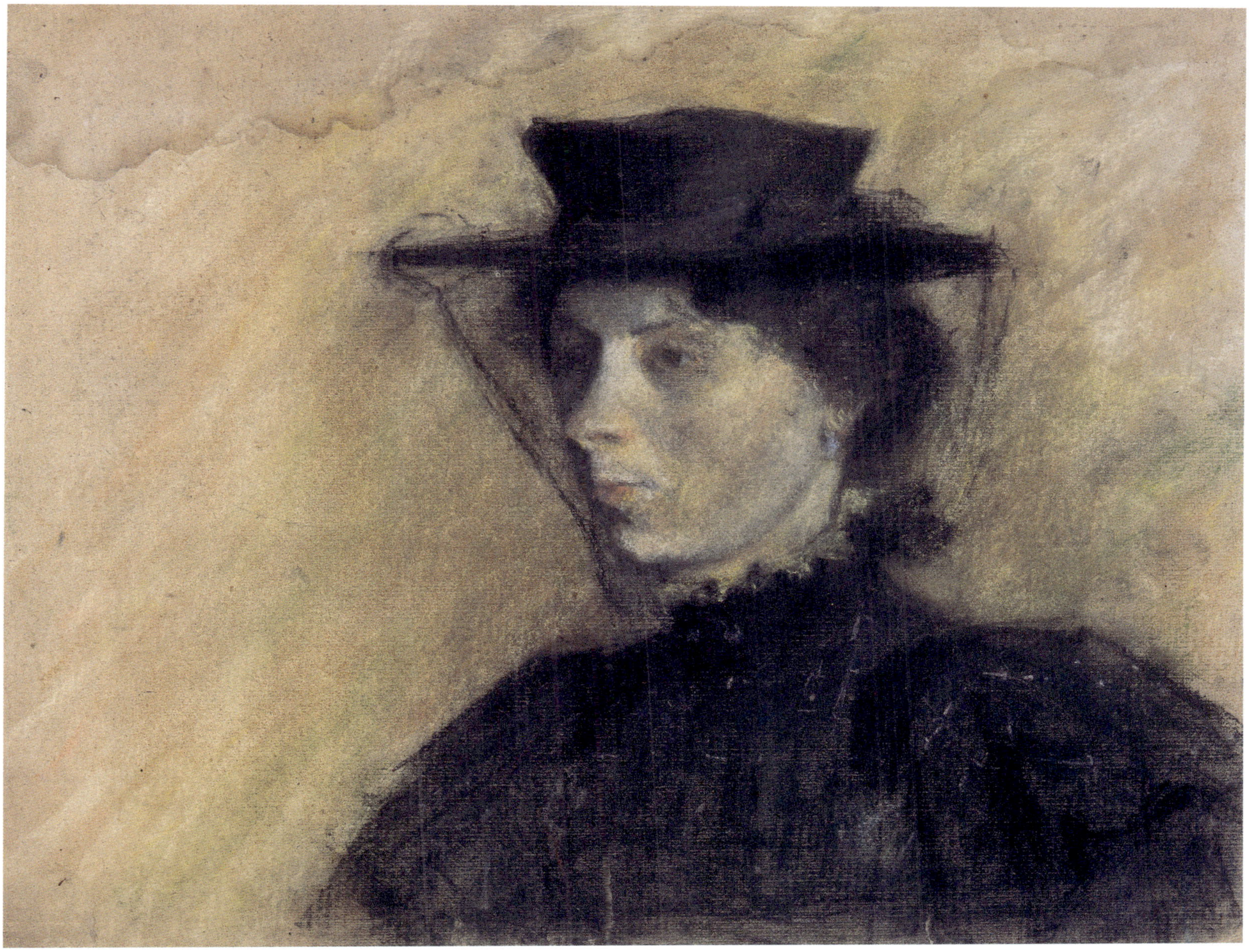

Portrait of a Lady Wearing a Hat and Veil, 1897

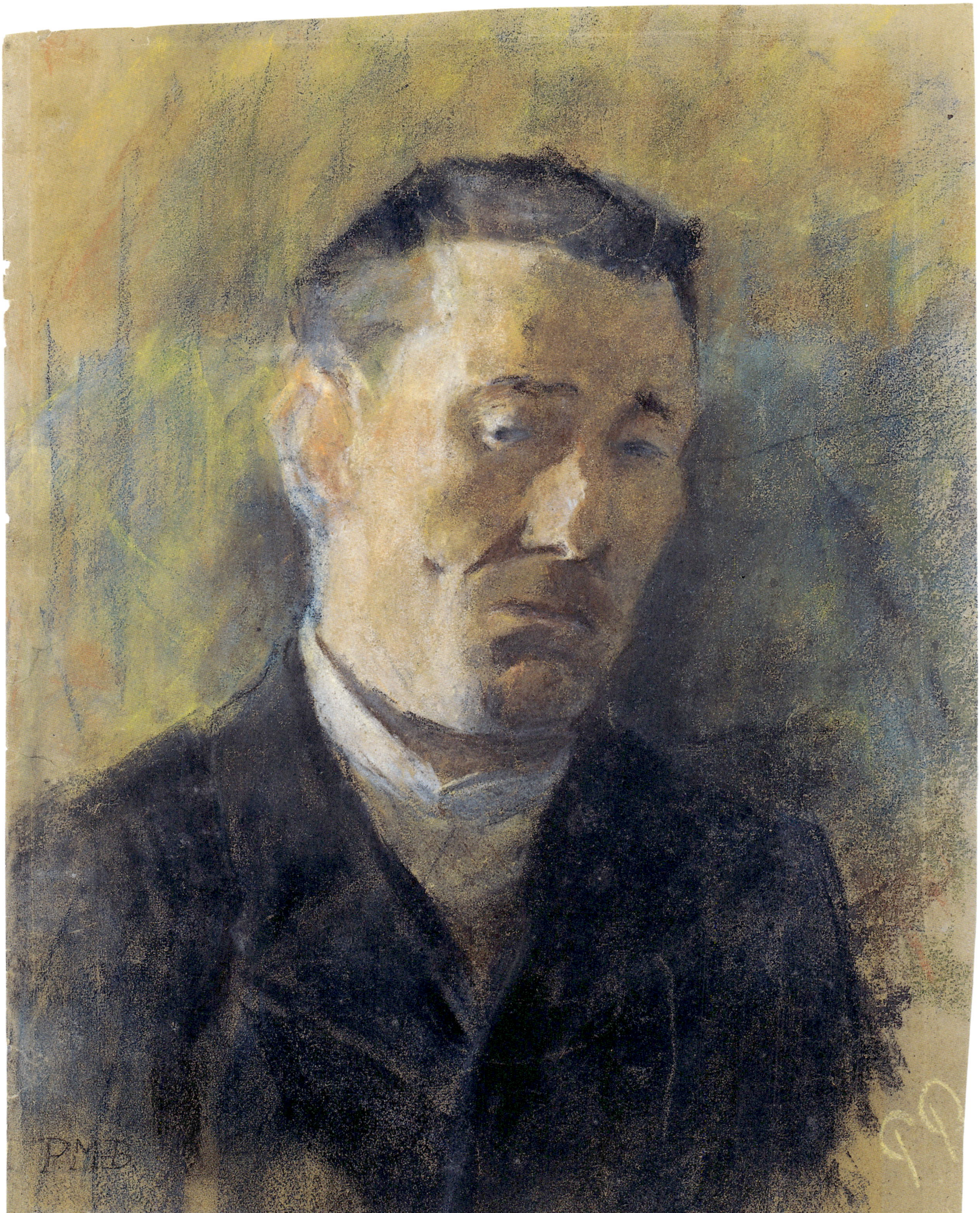

Bust Portrait of a Man Facing Half-Right, c. 1897

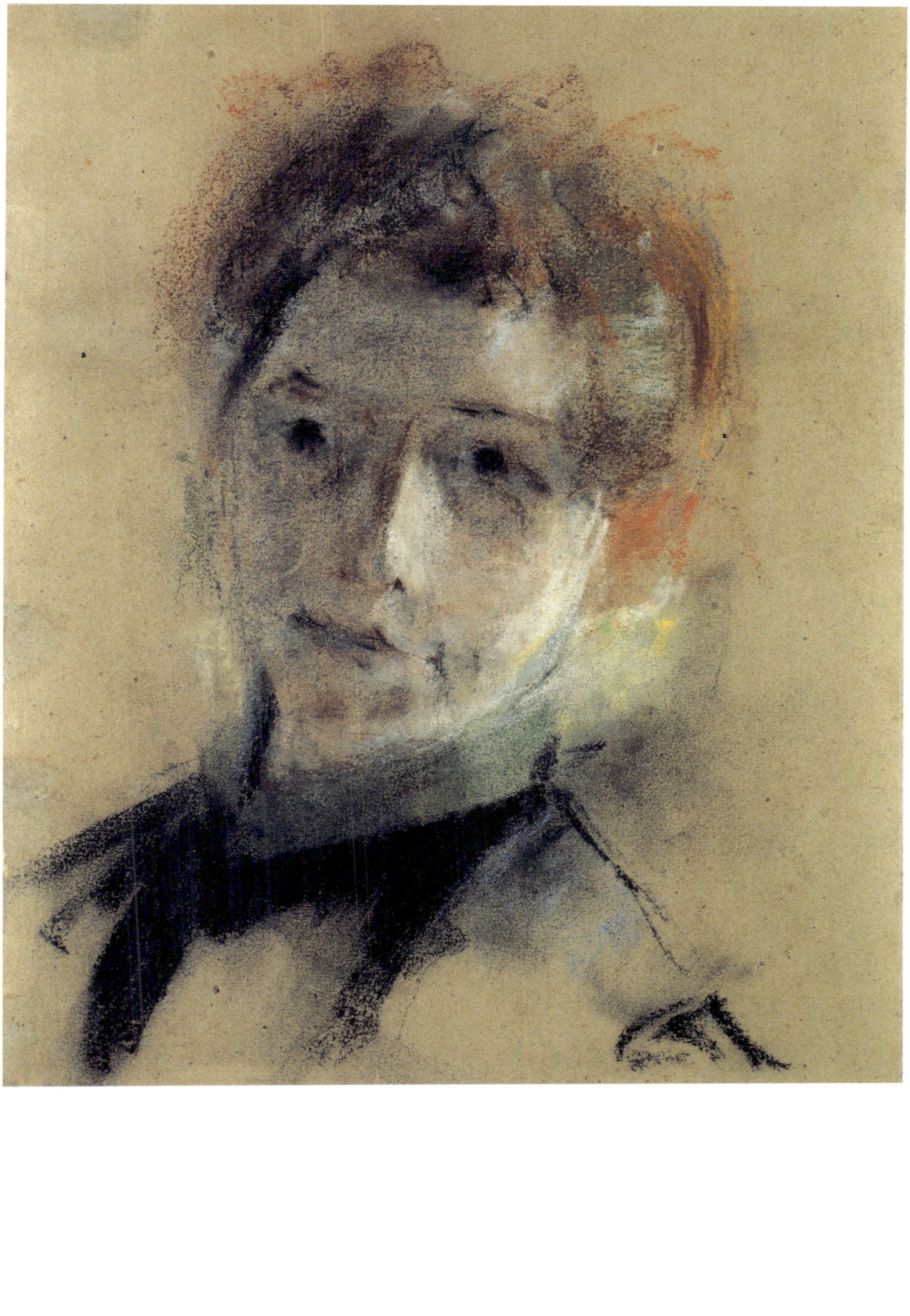

Self-Portrait, c. 1897

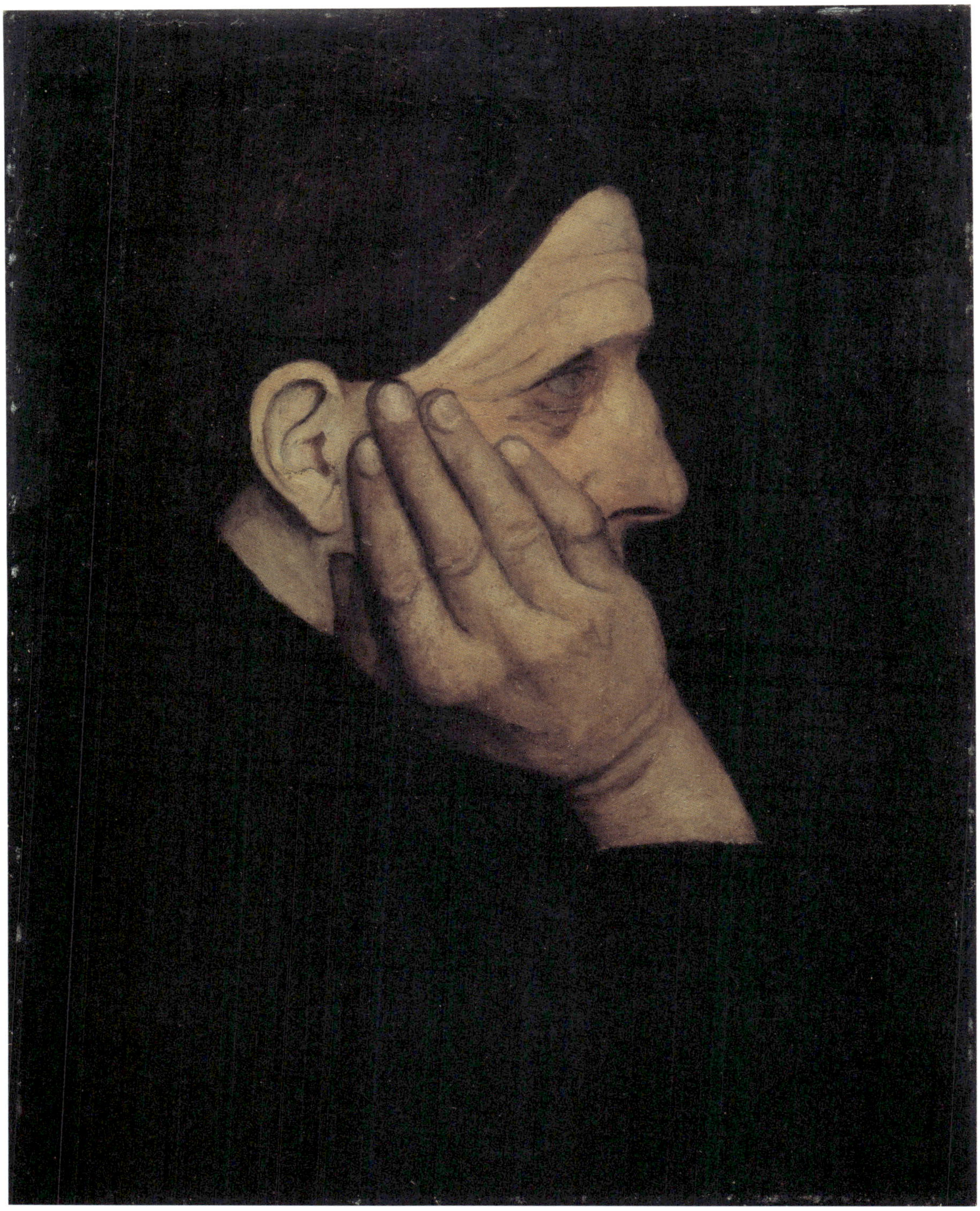

Bust Portrait of a Woman in Profile to the Right, c. 1898

Seated Old Blind Woman, 1898/99

9

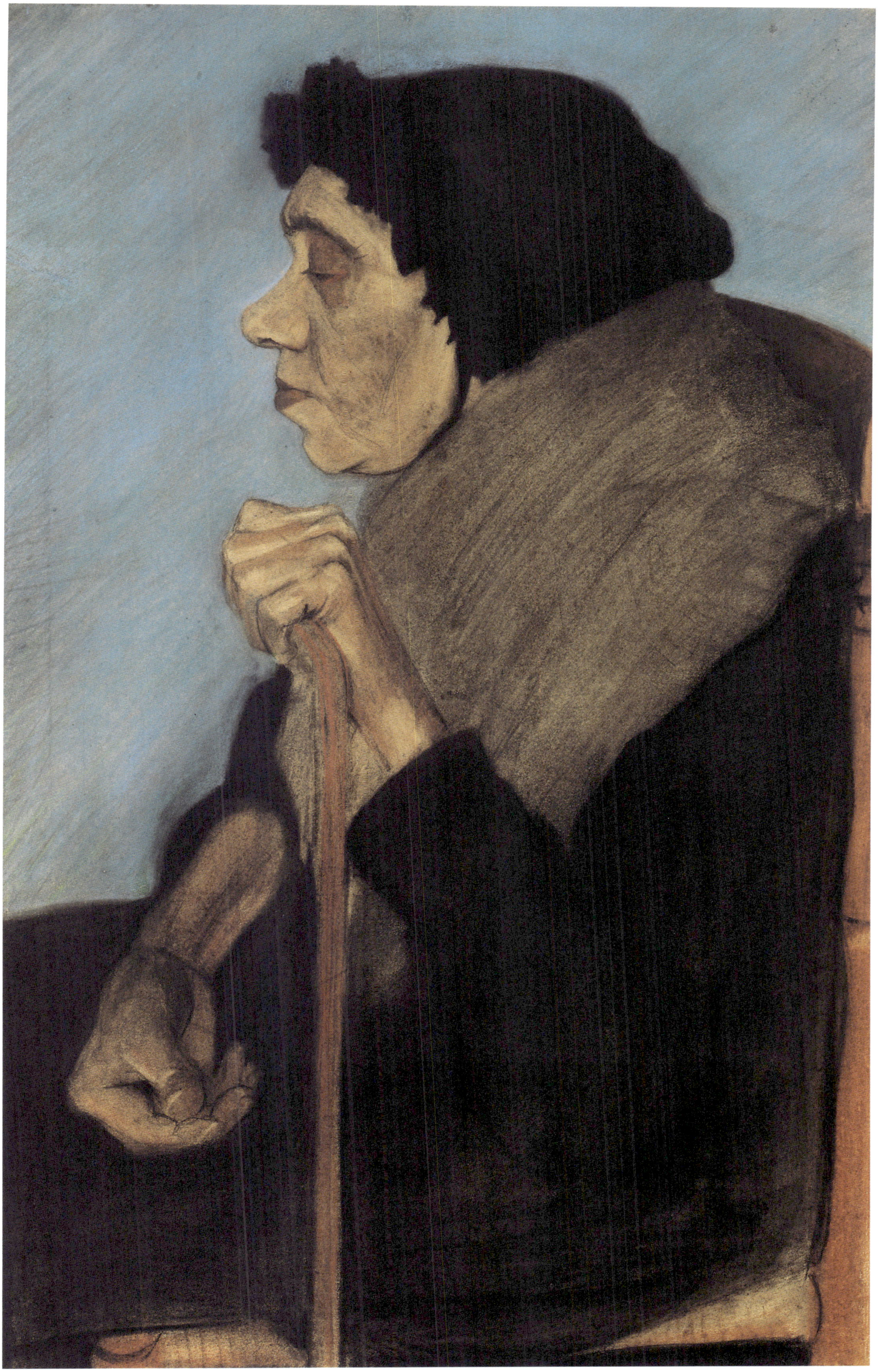

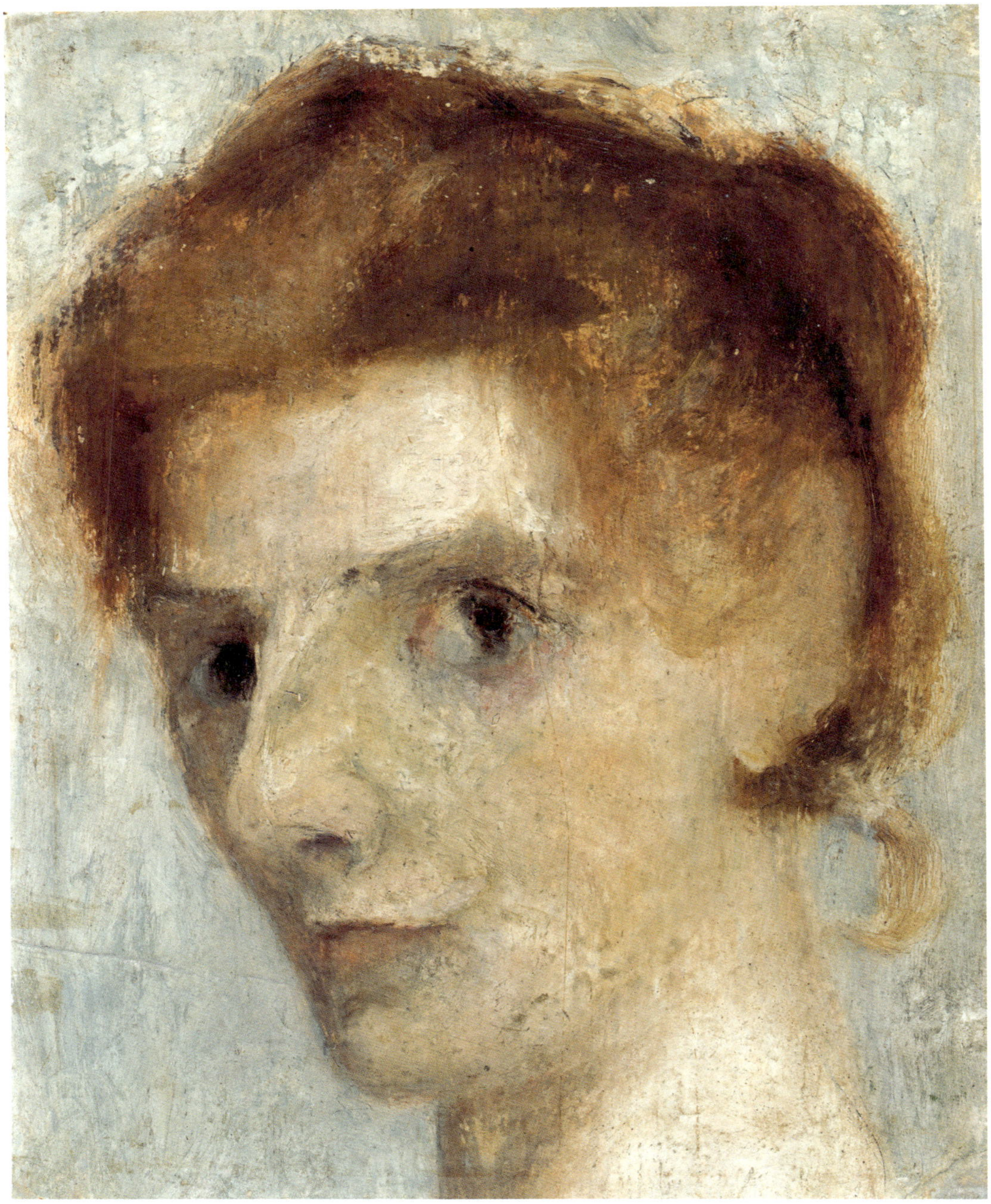

Self-Portrait, 1897/98

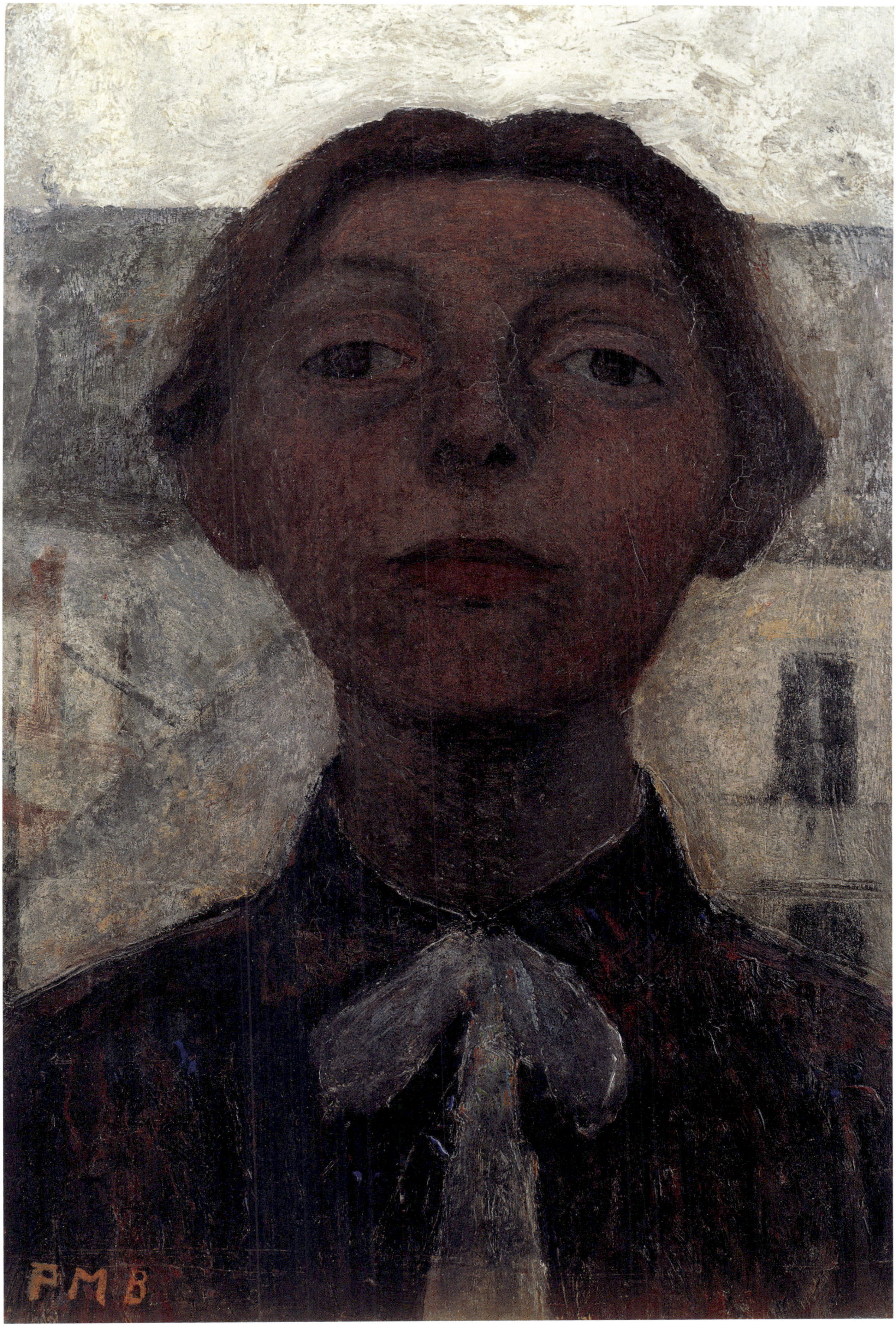

Self-Portrait with View from the Artist's Studio in Paris, 1900

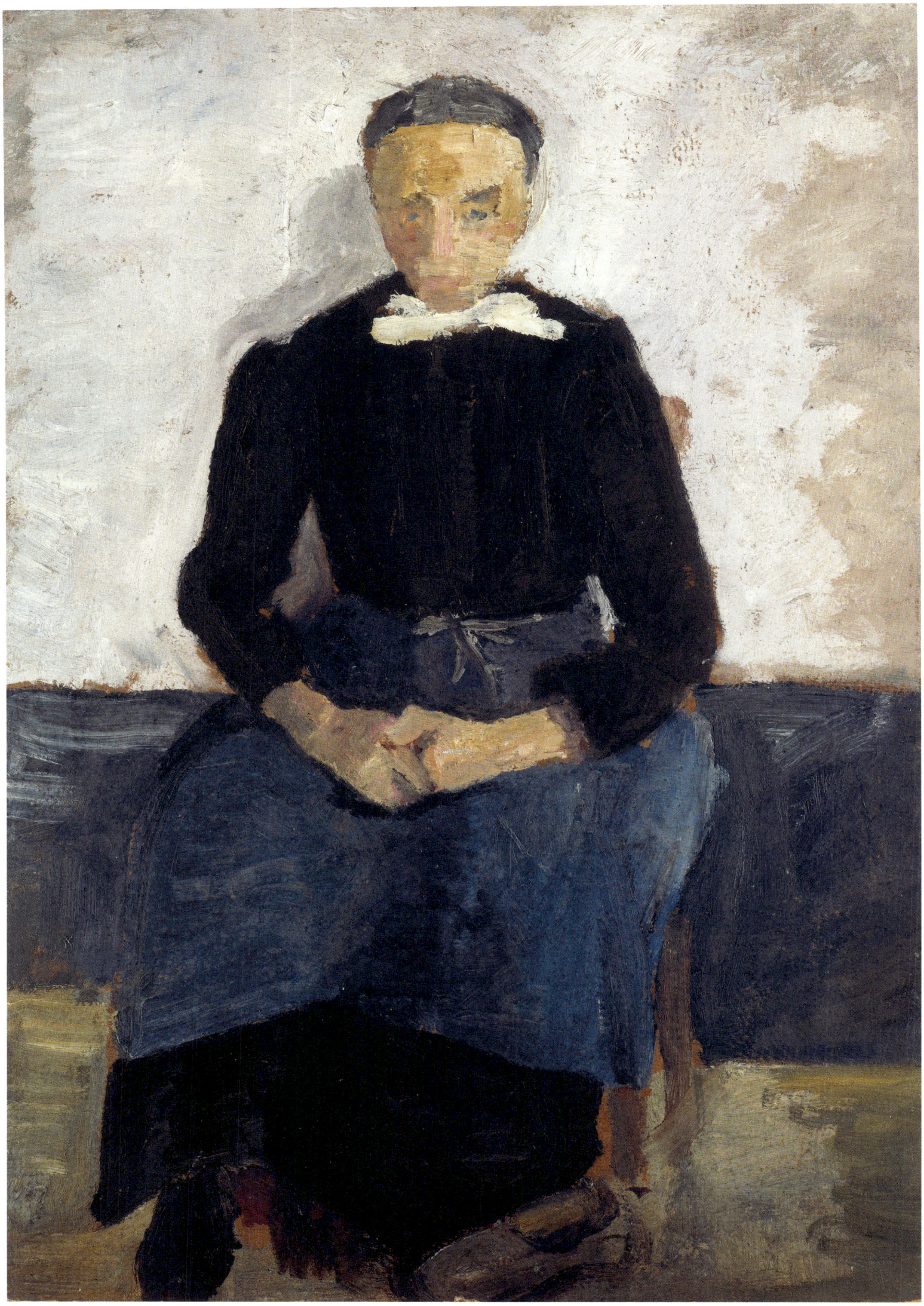

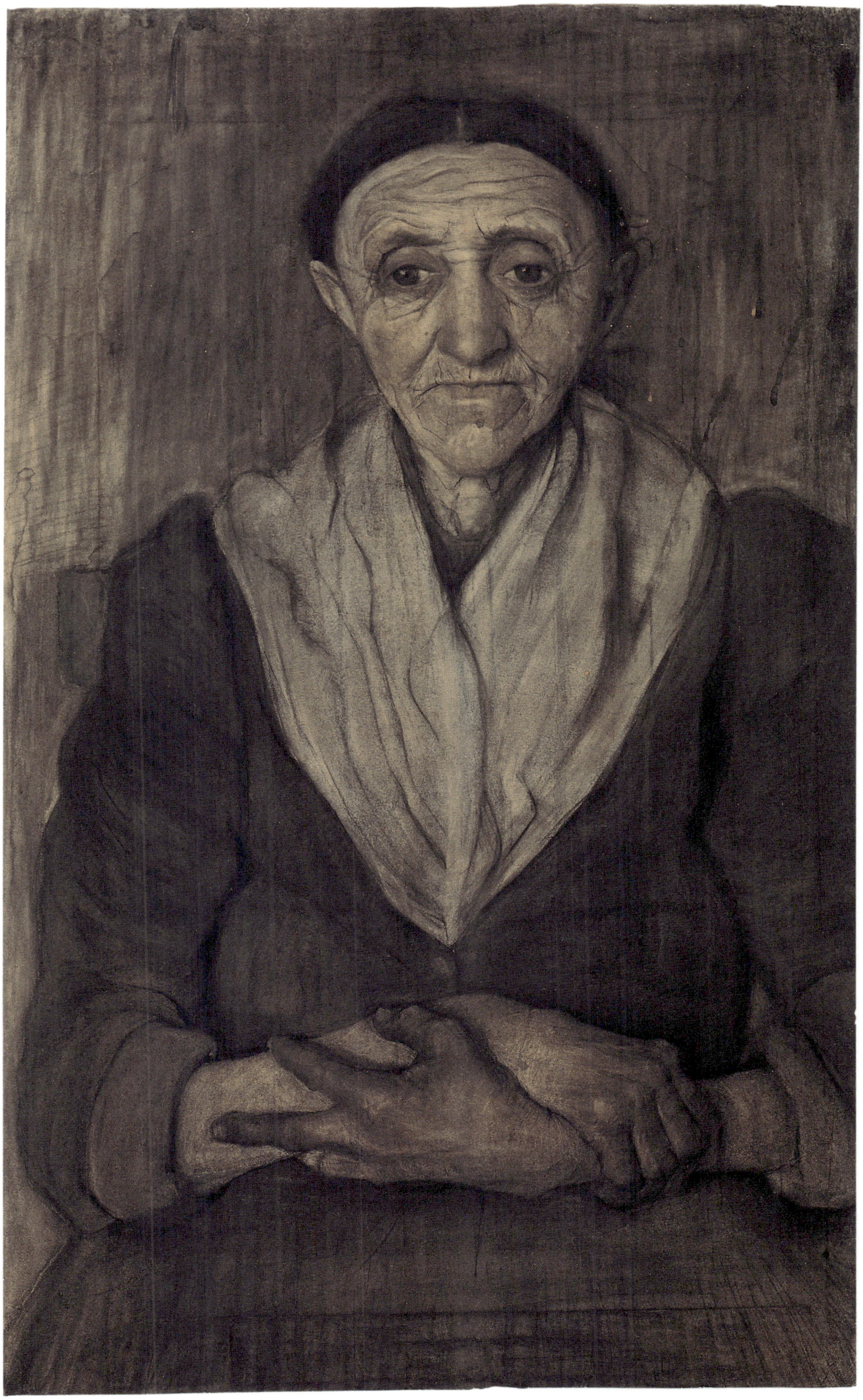

Woman with Hands Folded in Her Lap, 1898

Seated Old Woman, Her Hands in Her Lap, 1898/99

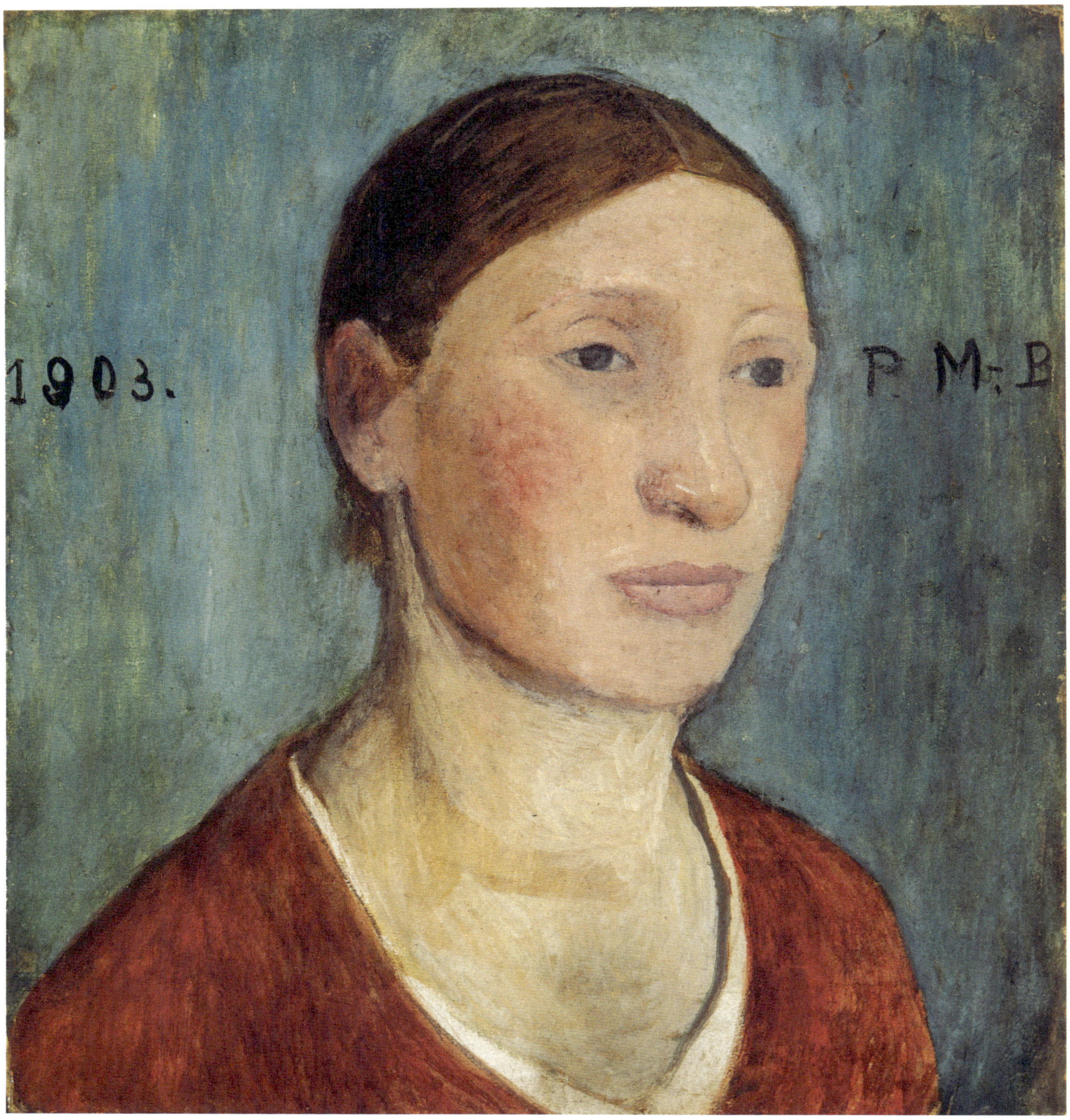

Bust Portrait of a Farm Woman in a Red Dress, 1903

Seated Old Woman with Handkerchief, c. 1903

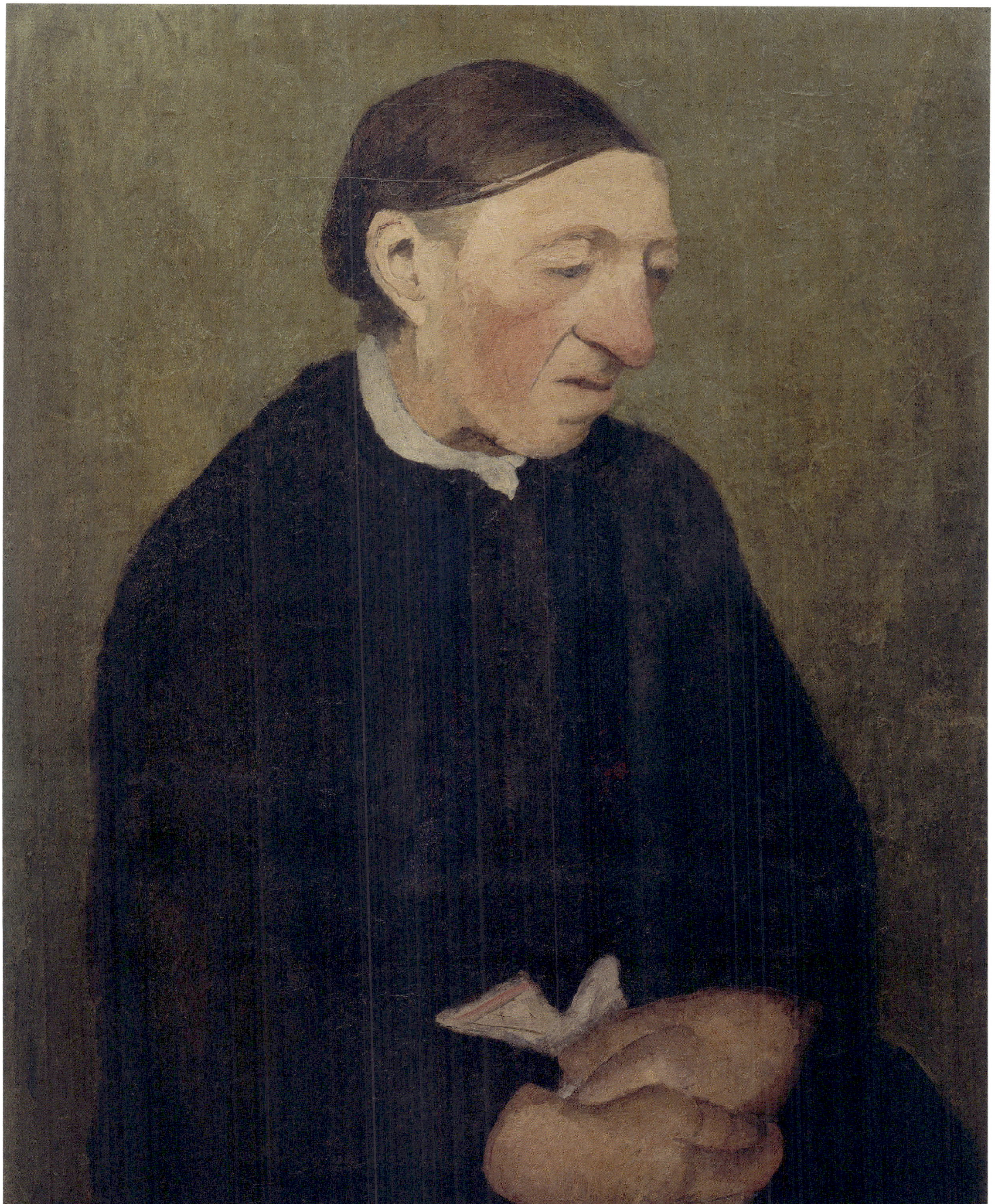

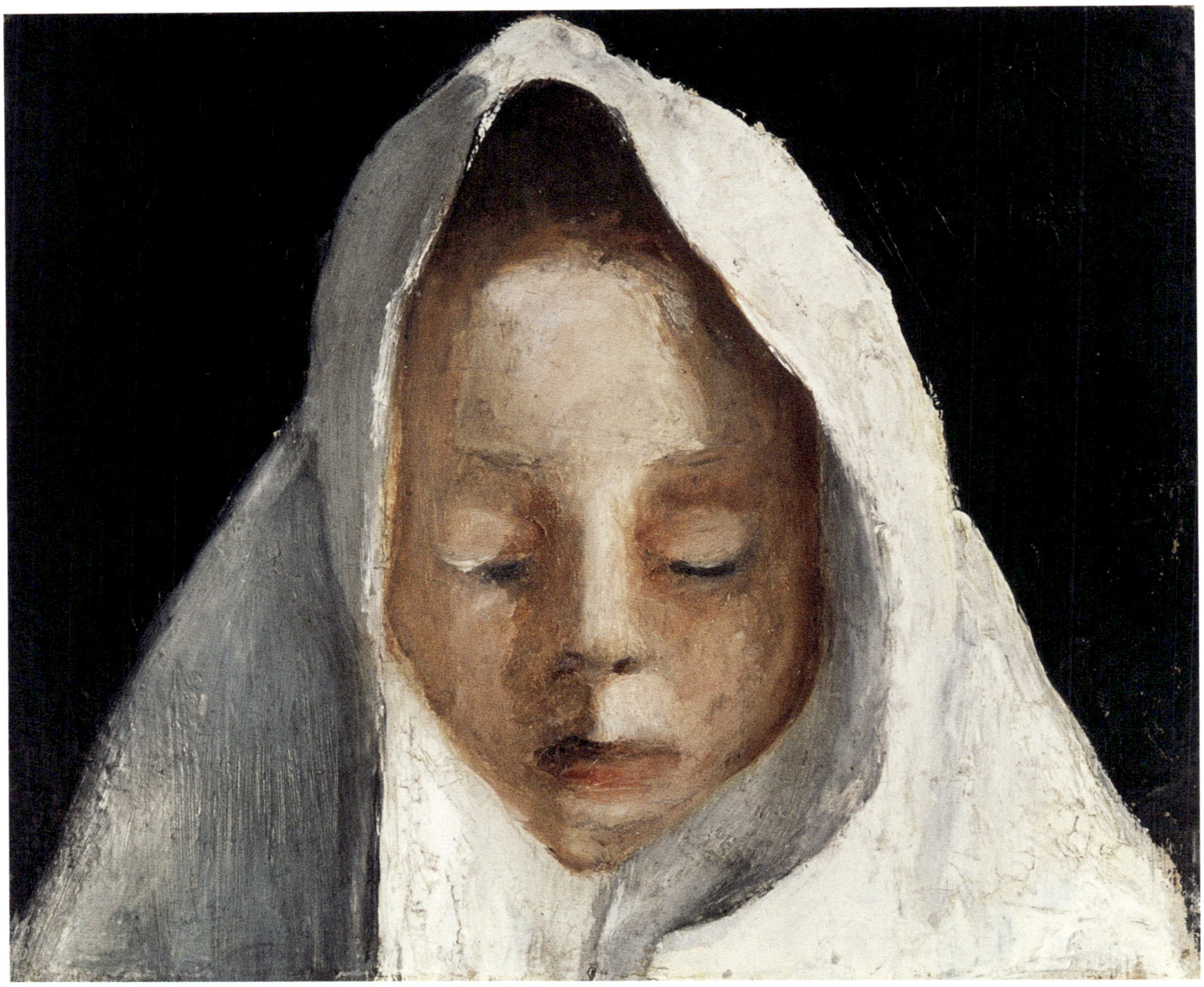

Child's Head with White Cloth, c. 1897

Bust Portrait of an Old Woman with White Cloth, 1897

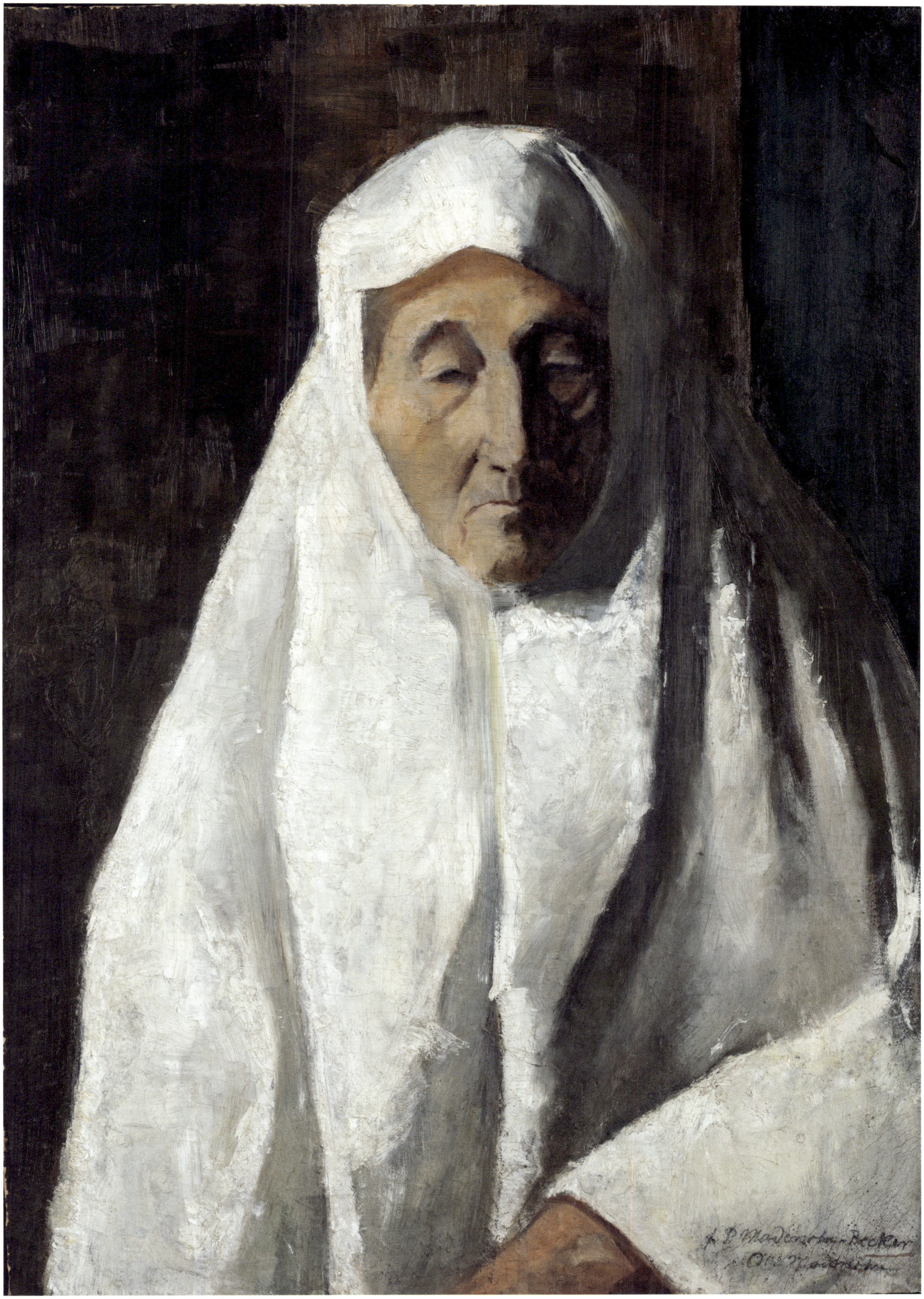

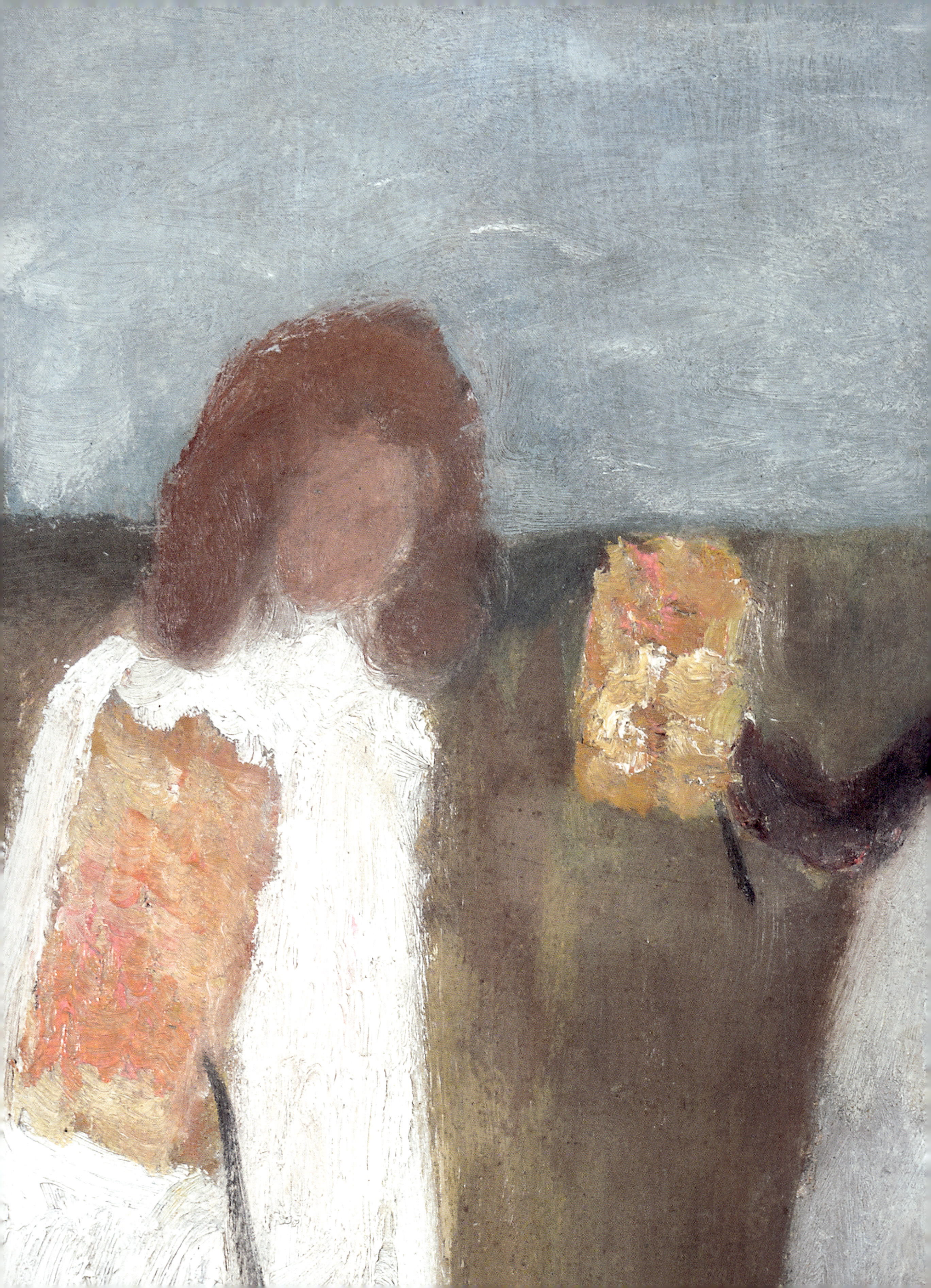

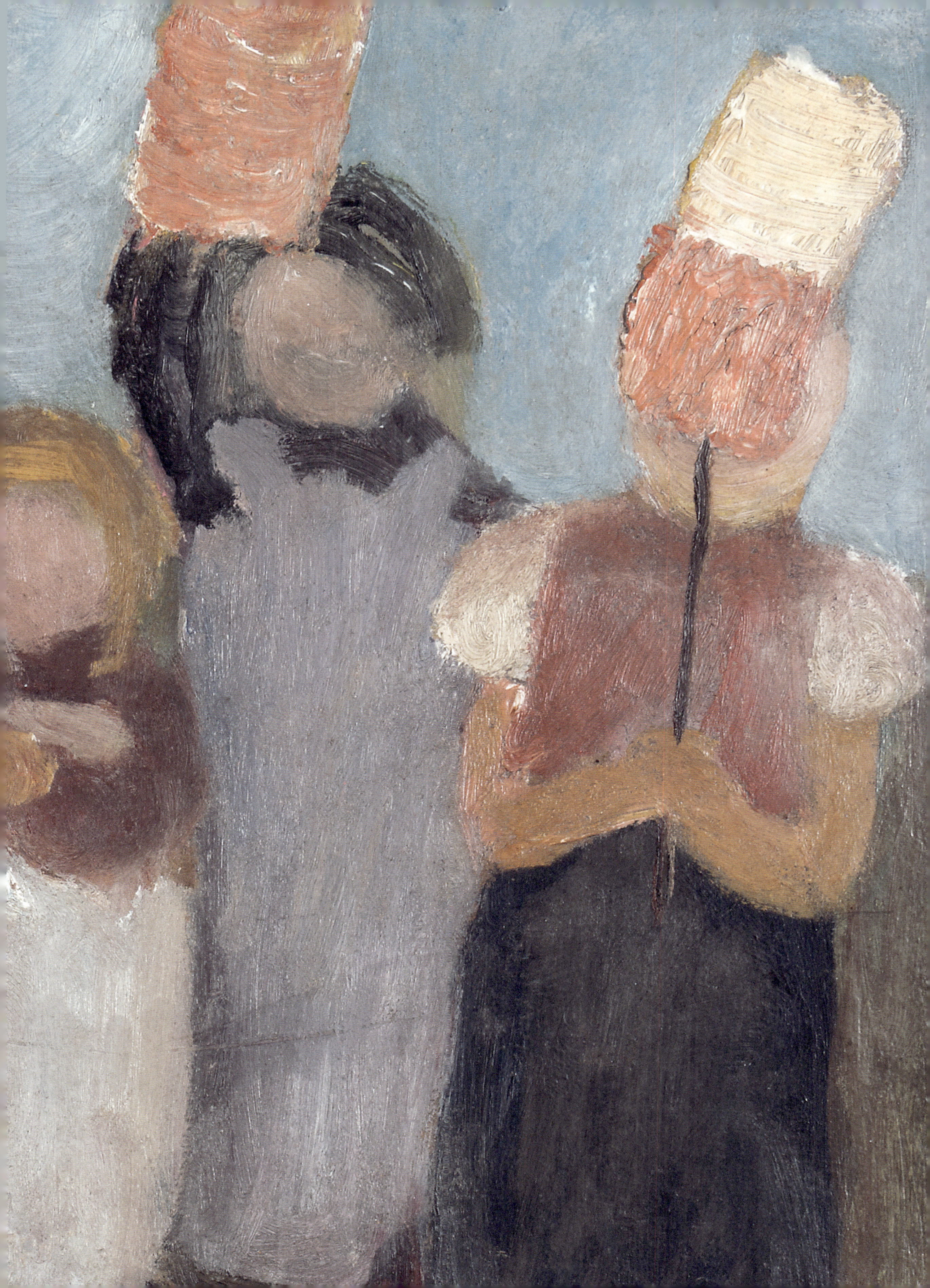

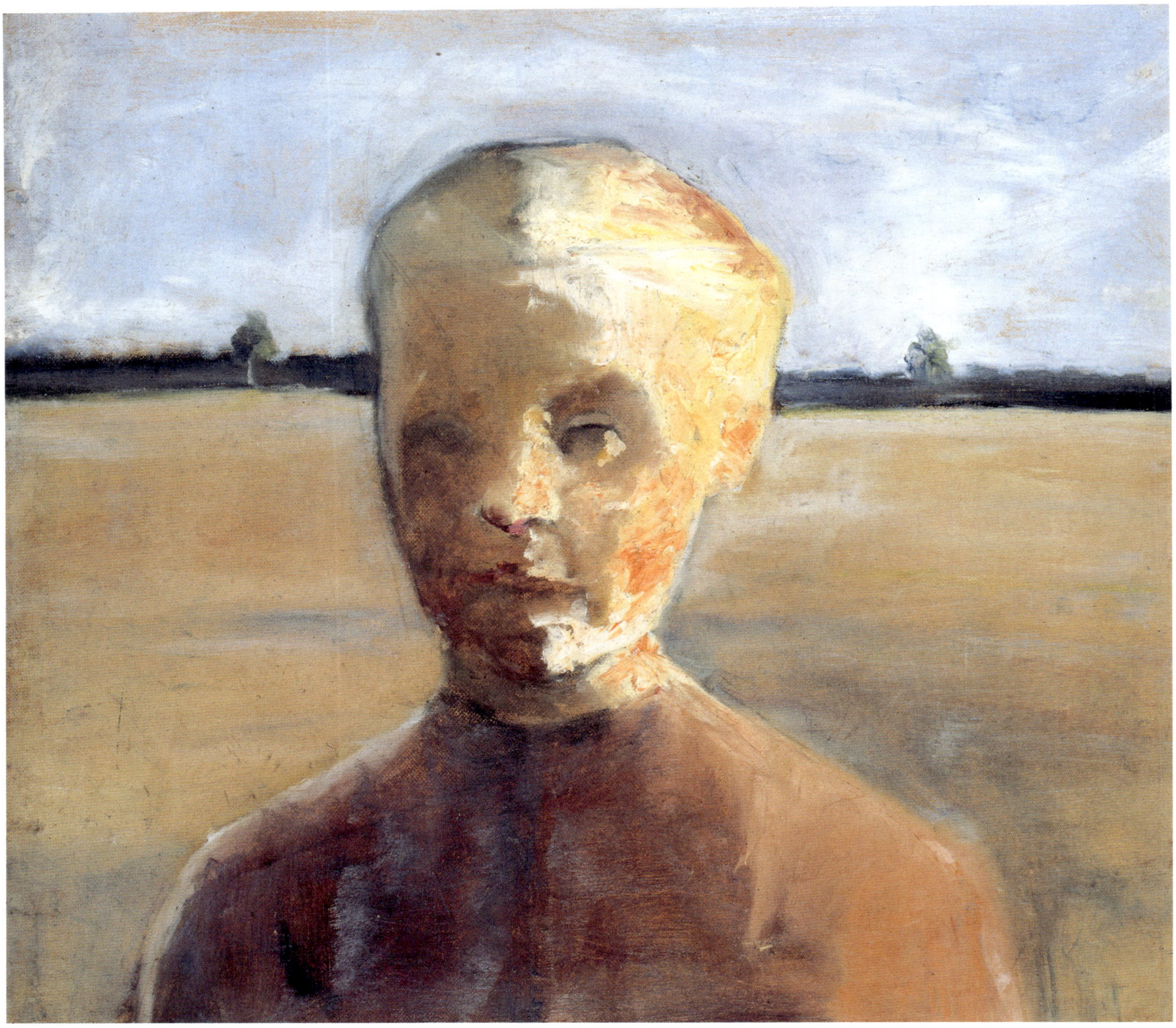

Bust Portrait of a Girl in the Sun in front of a Wide Landscape, 1897

Children with Lanterns in front of a House, 1901

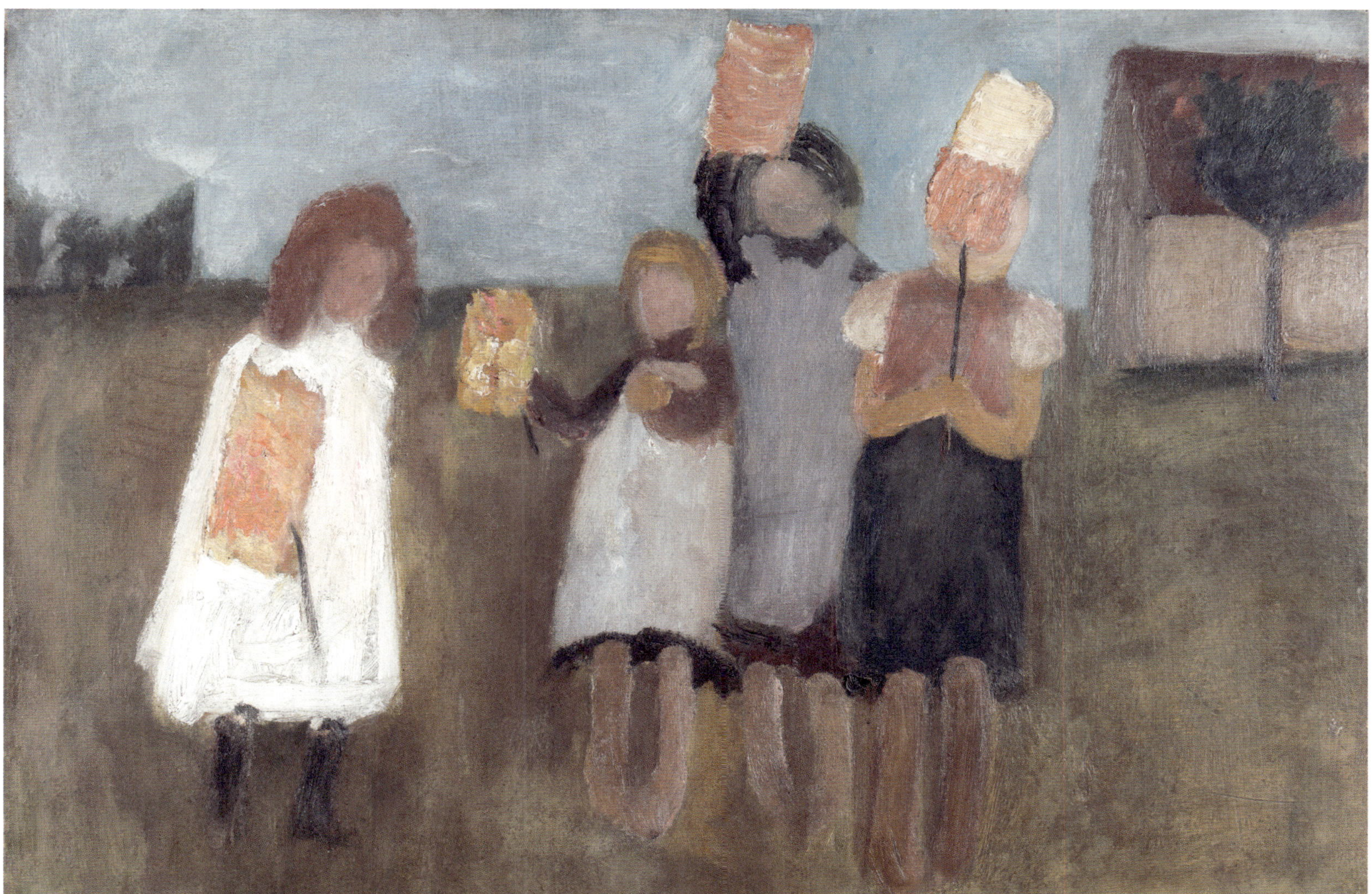

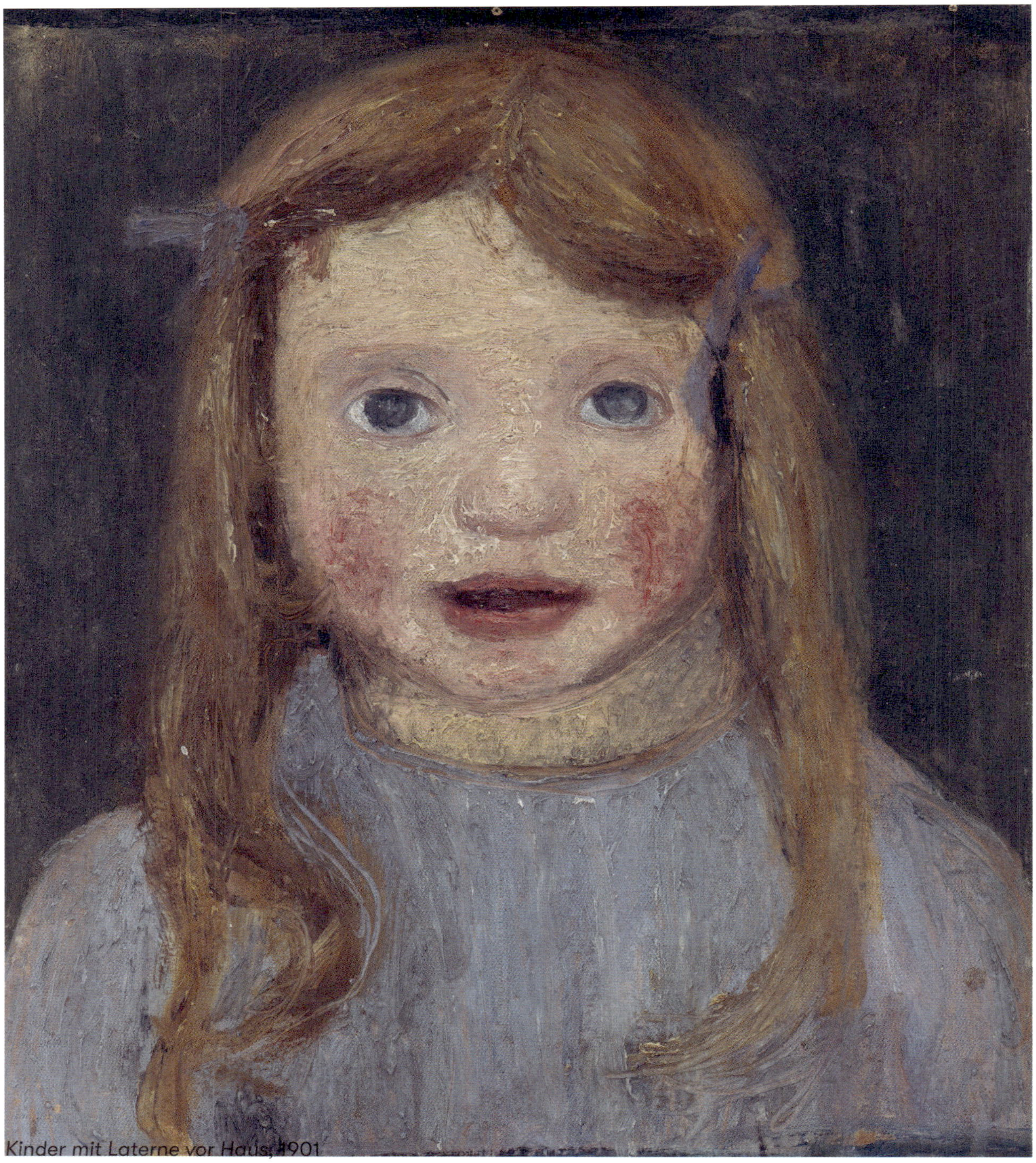

Kinder mit Laterne vor Haus, 1901

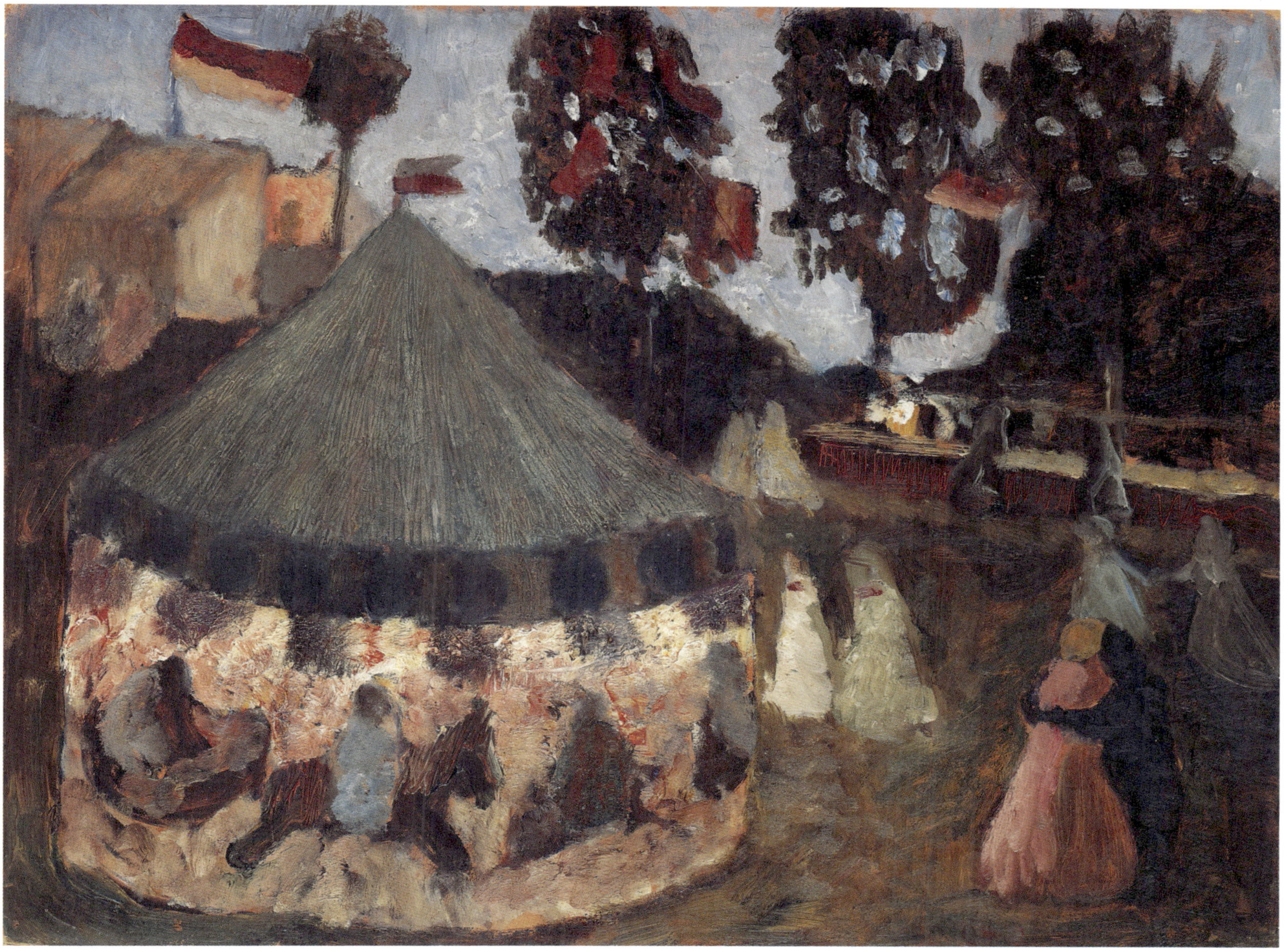

Elsbeth, c. 1902

Shooting Festival with Carousel II, 1904

Moon over Landscape, c. 1900

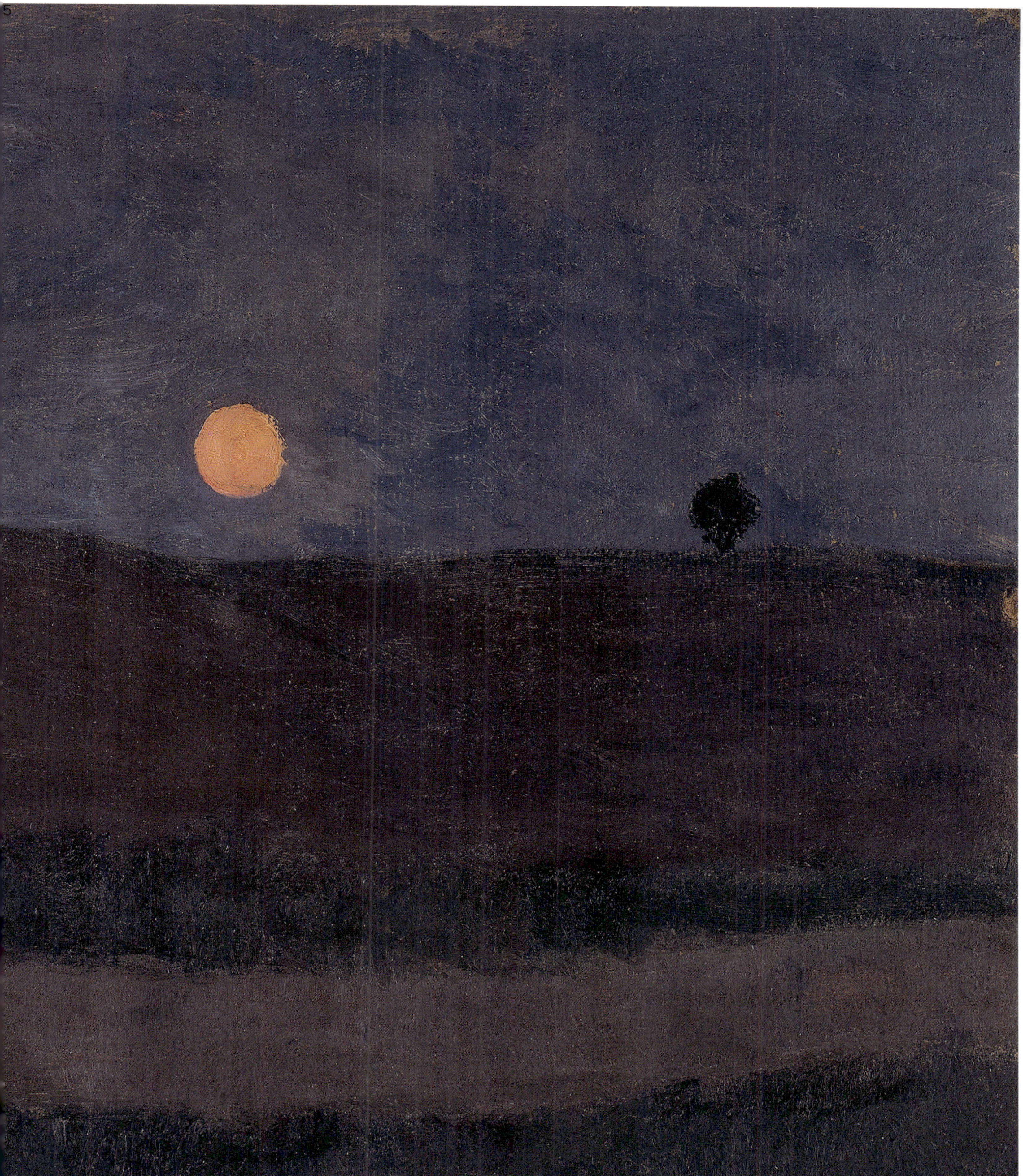

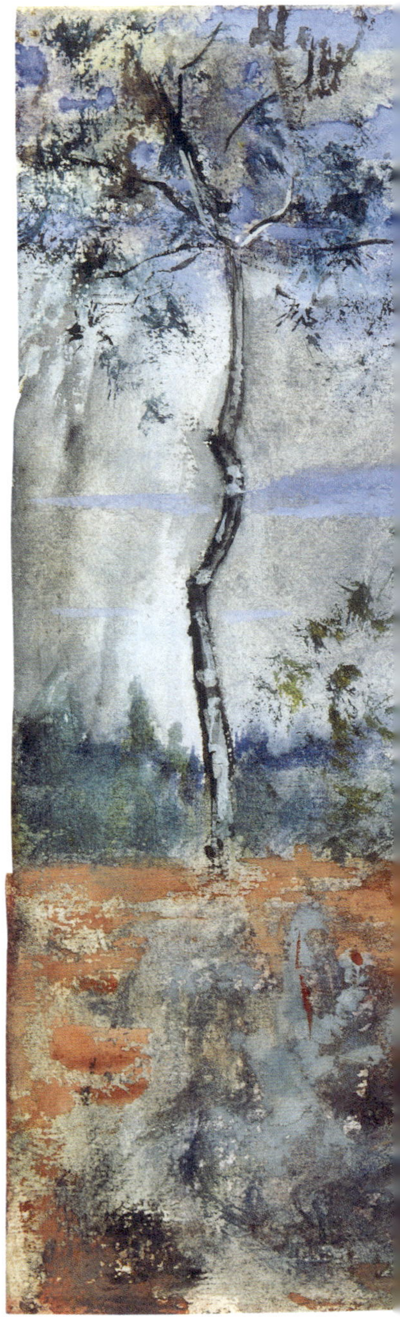

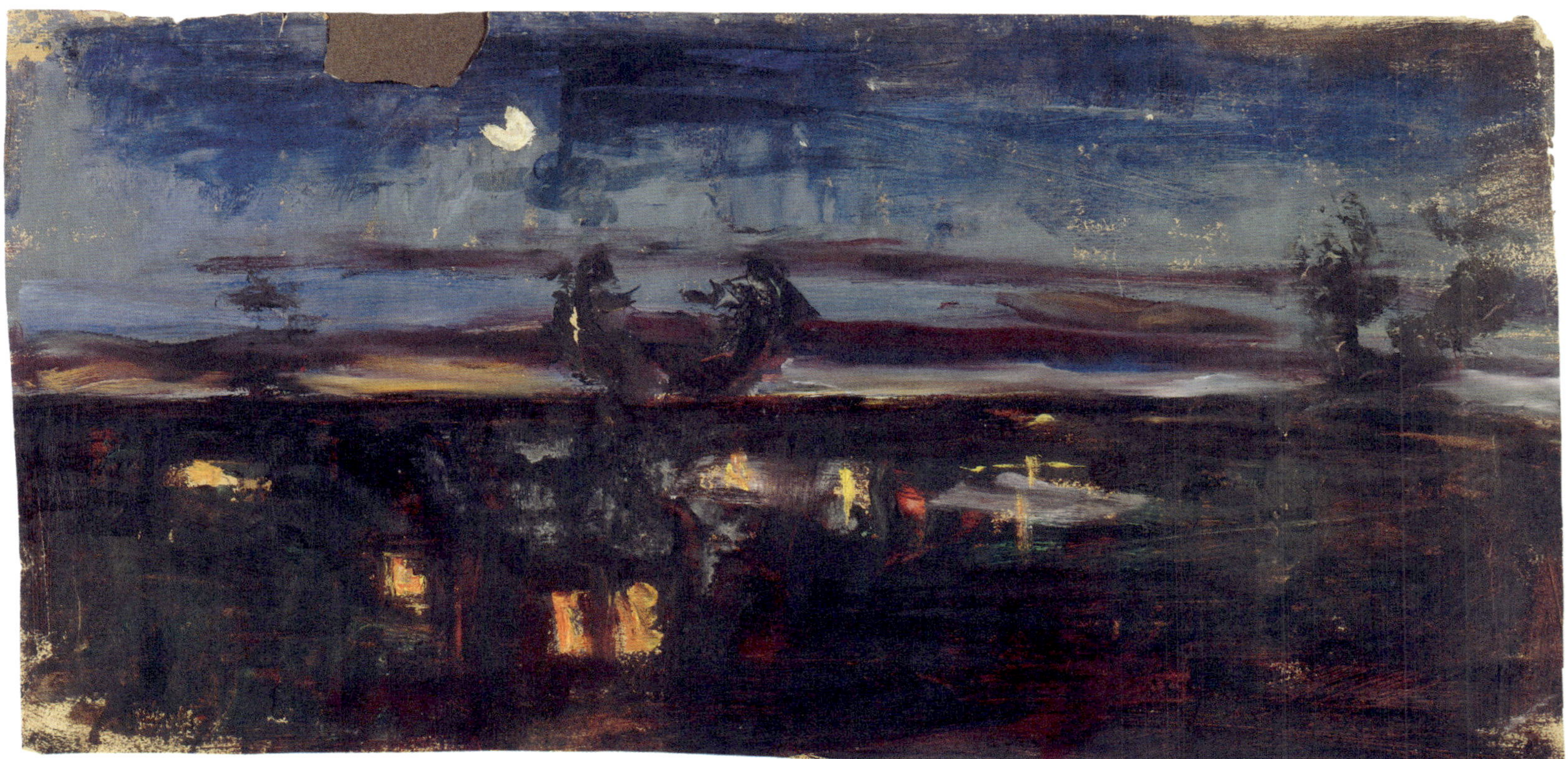

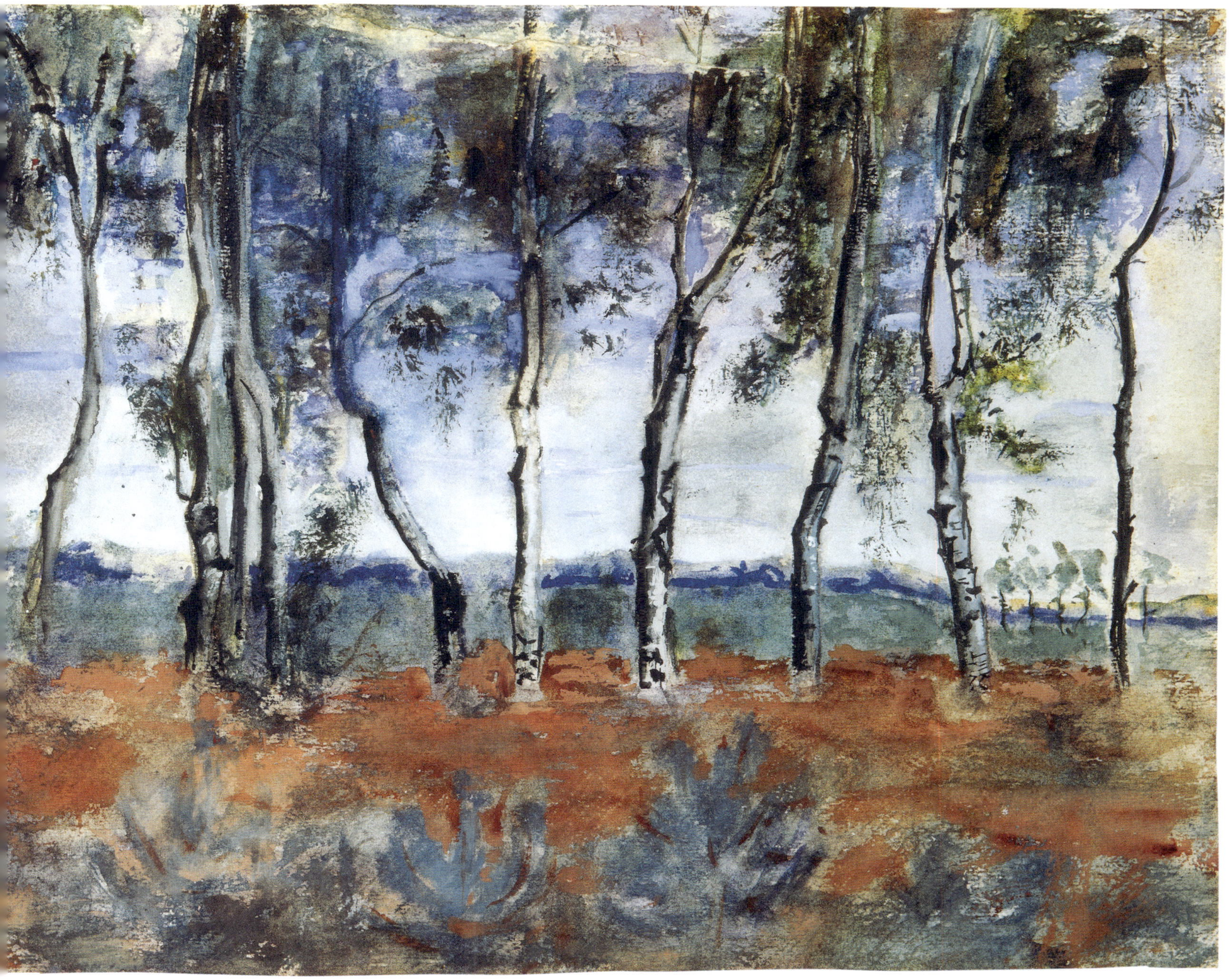

Night-Time Landscape, 1897

Row of Trees, 1897

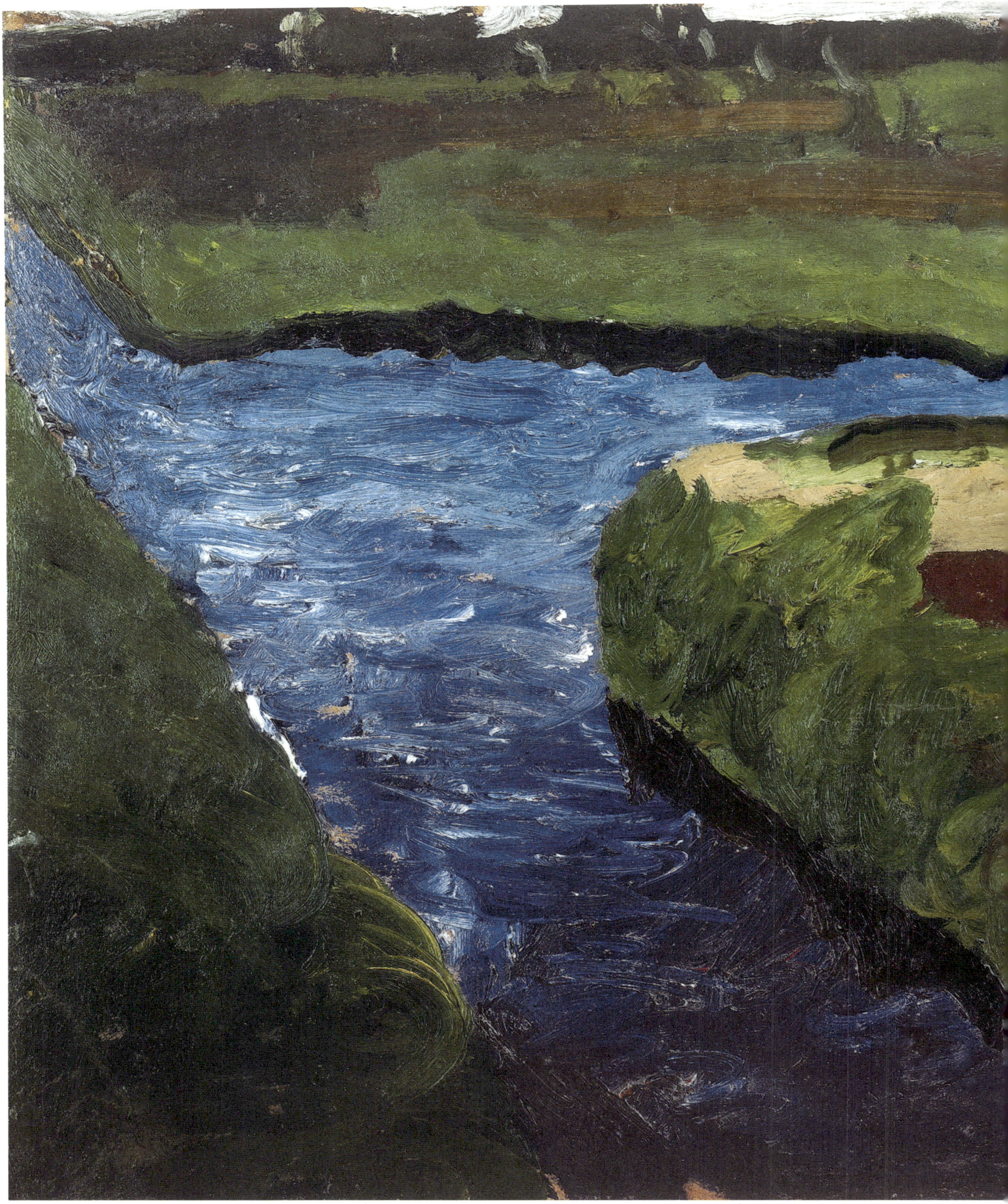

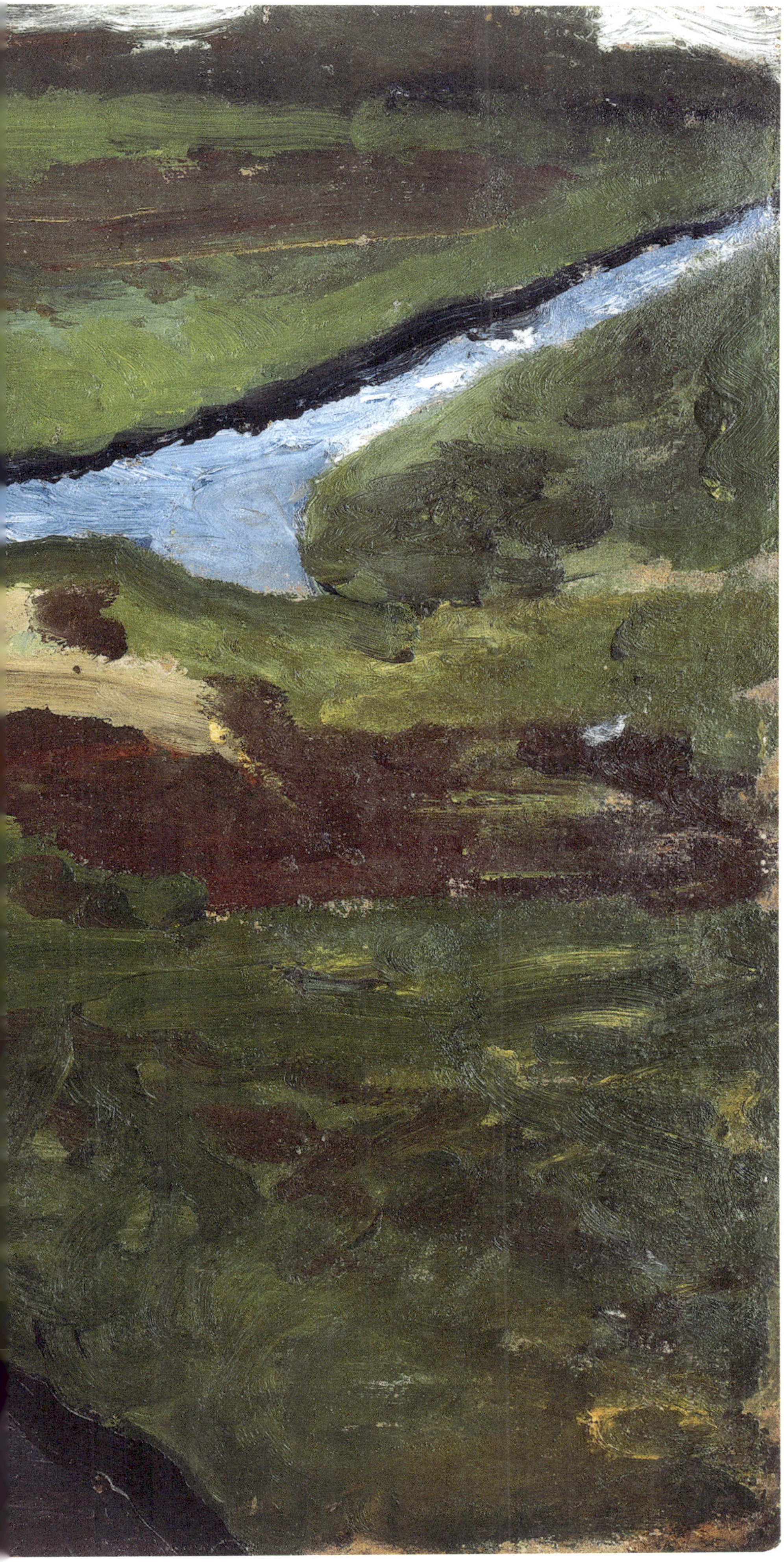

Moor Ditch, 1900

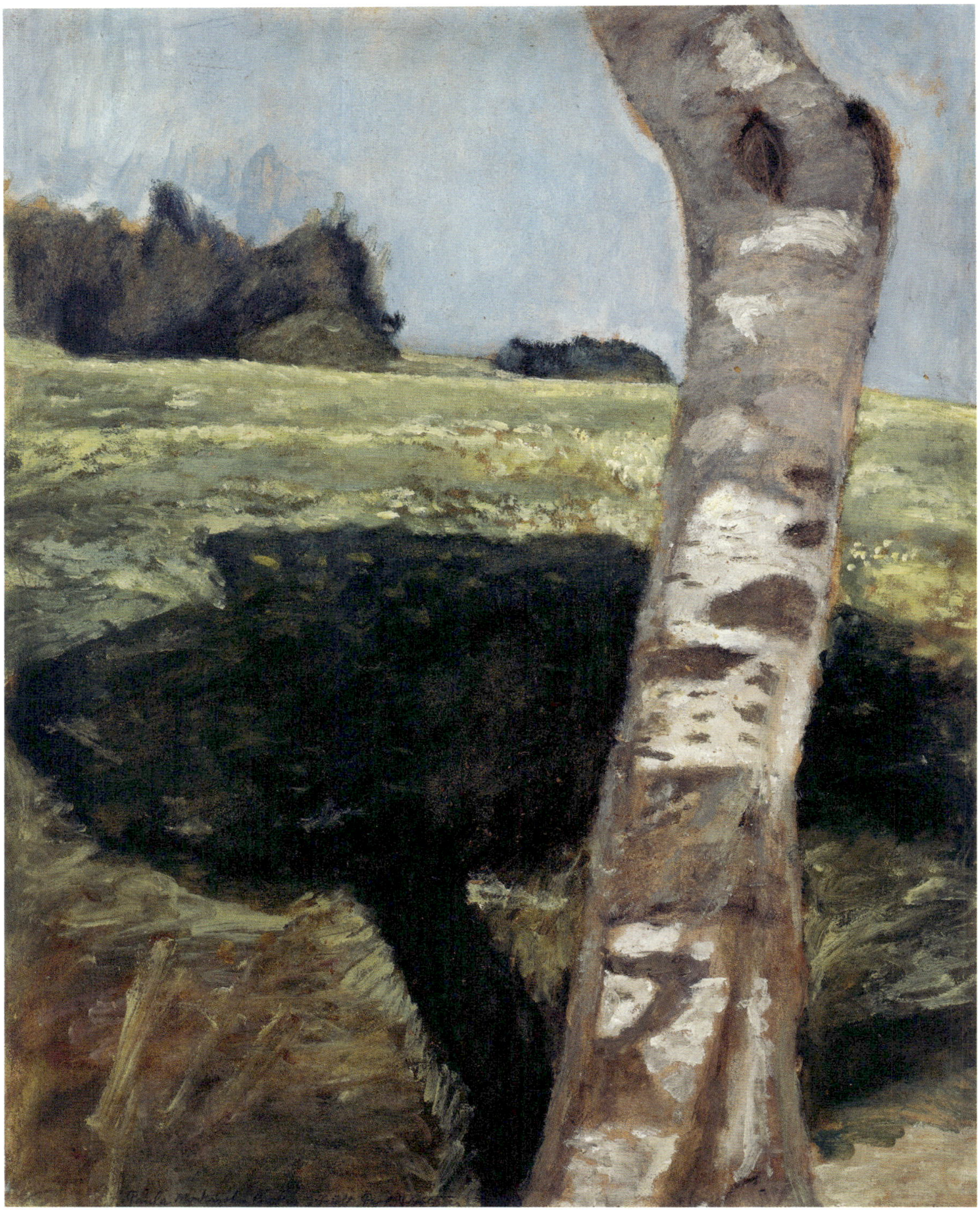

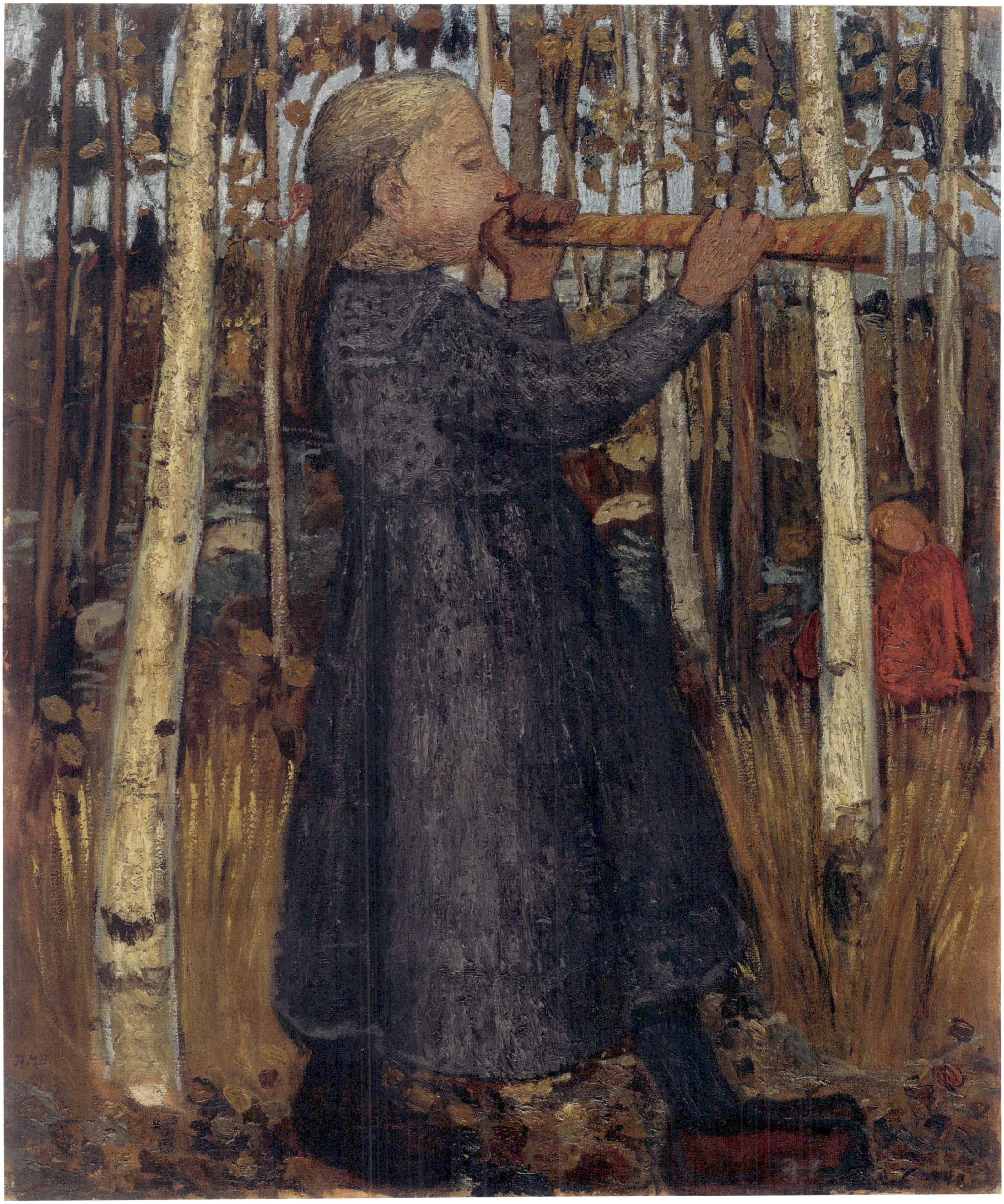

Birch Trunk in front of a Landscape, c. 1903

Girl Playing the Flute in a Birch Forest, 1905

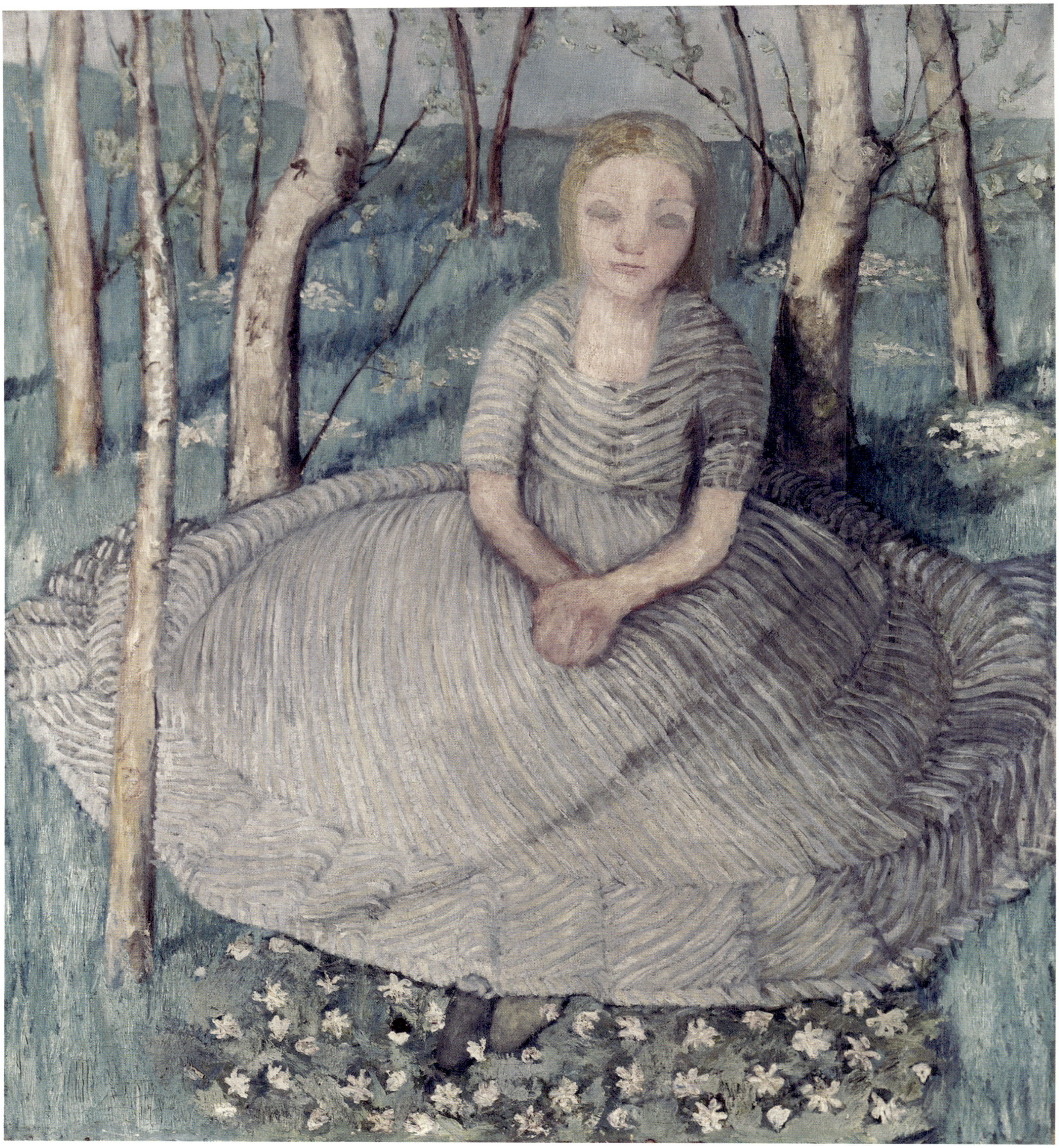

Girl Sitting among Trees in a Meadow with Blooming Windflowers, c. 1901

Child on a Red-Patterned Cushion, c. 1904

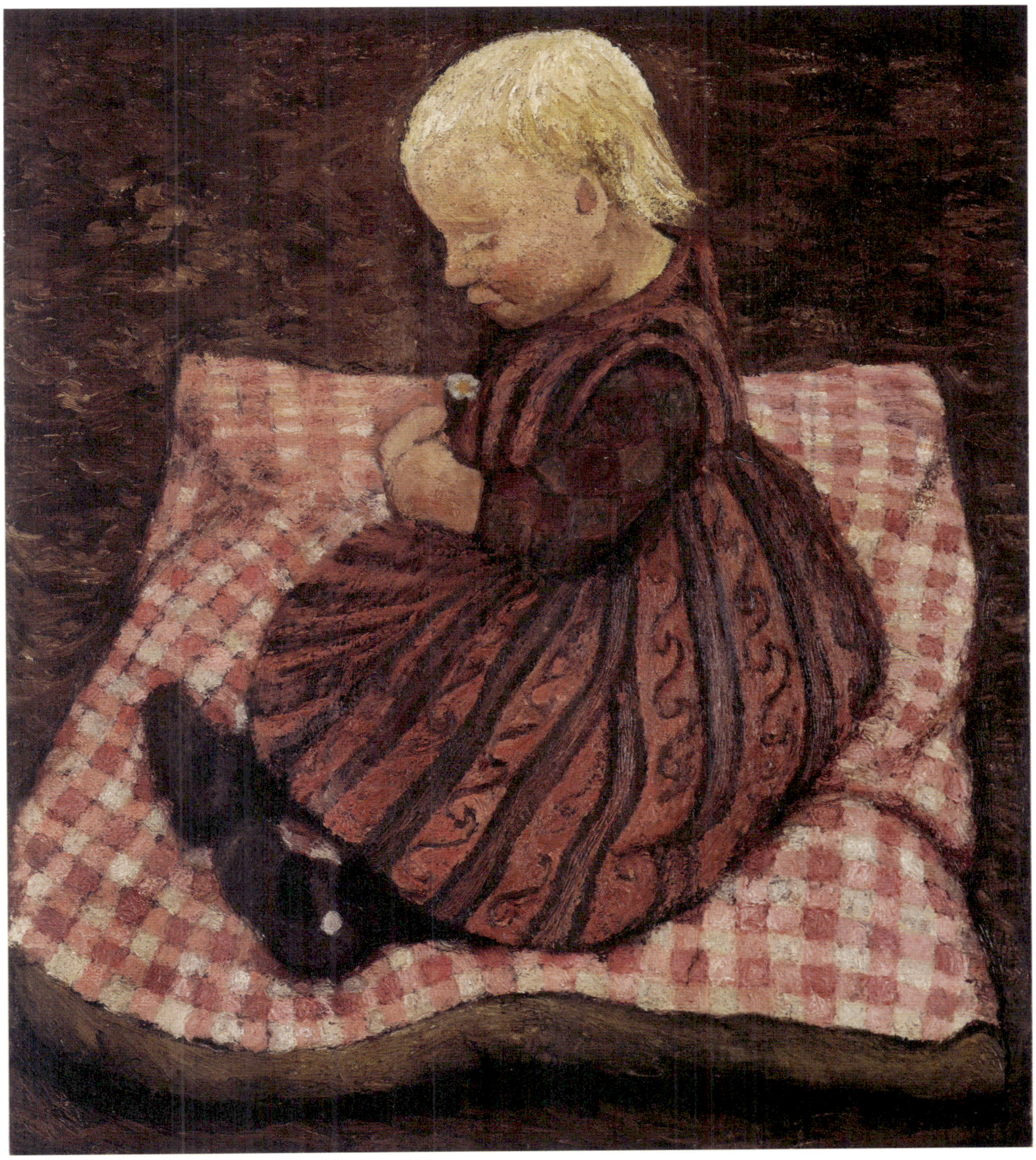

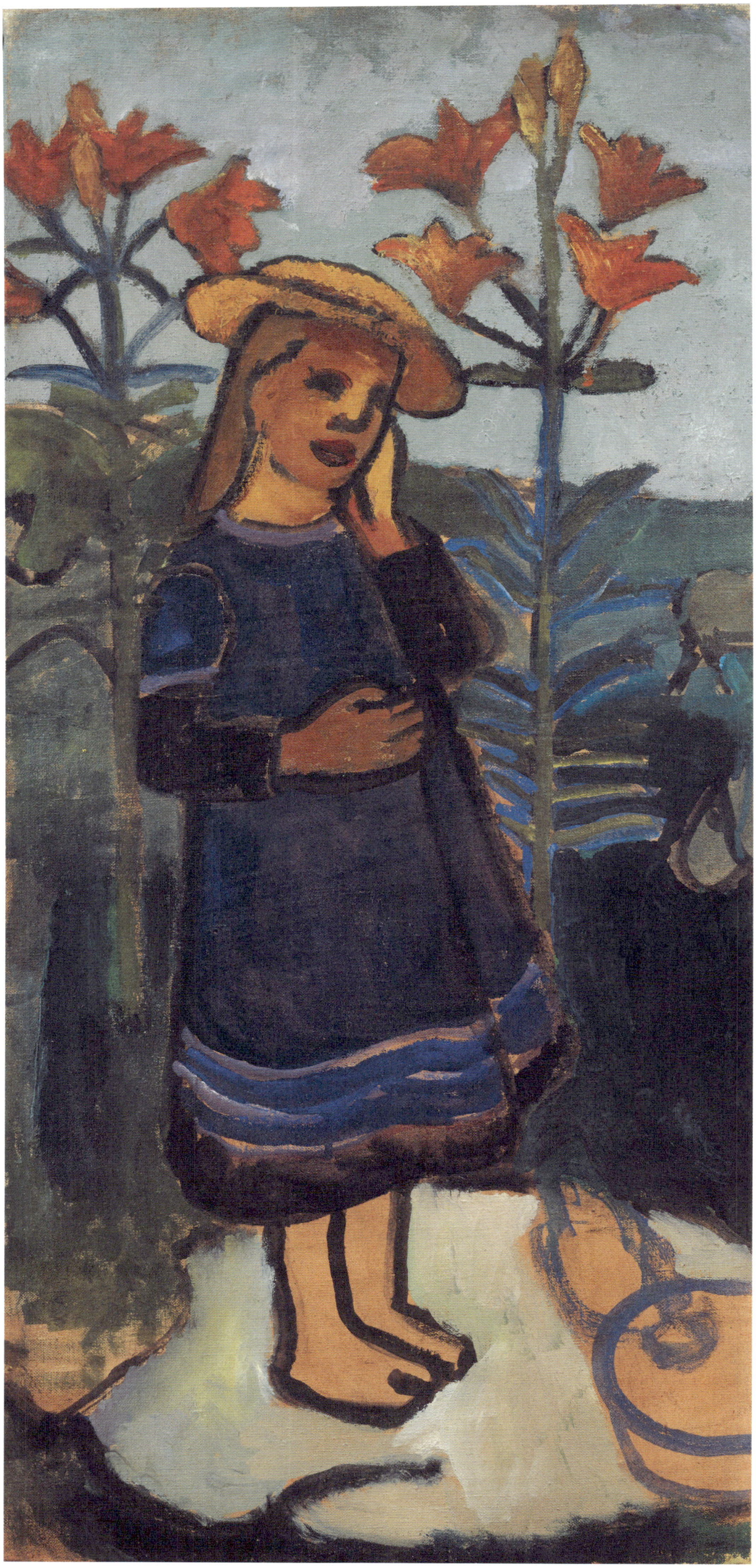

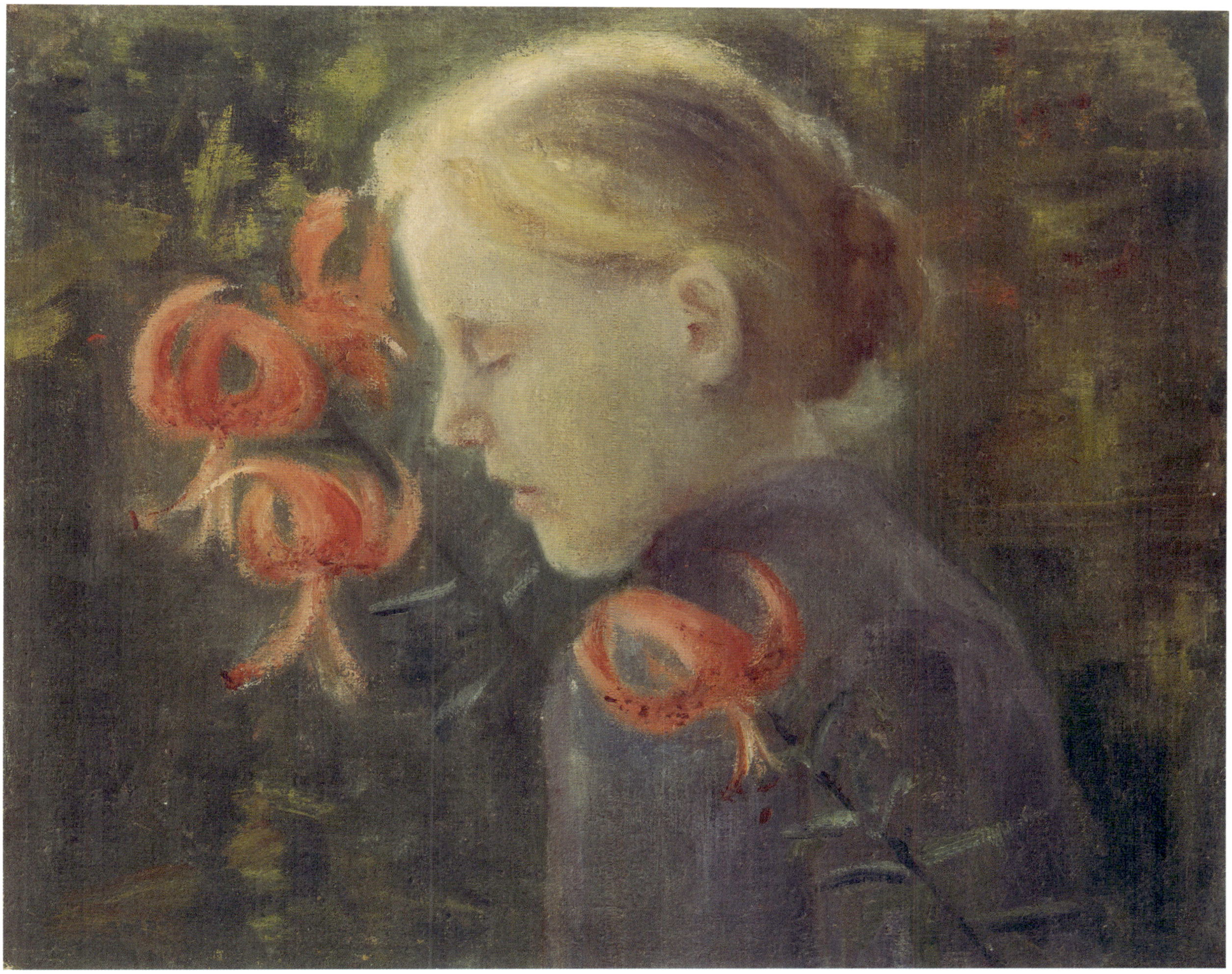

Elsbeth between Fire Lillies, 1907

Girl with Fire Lilies, 1897

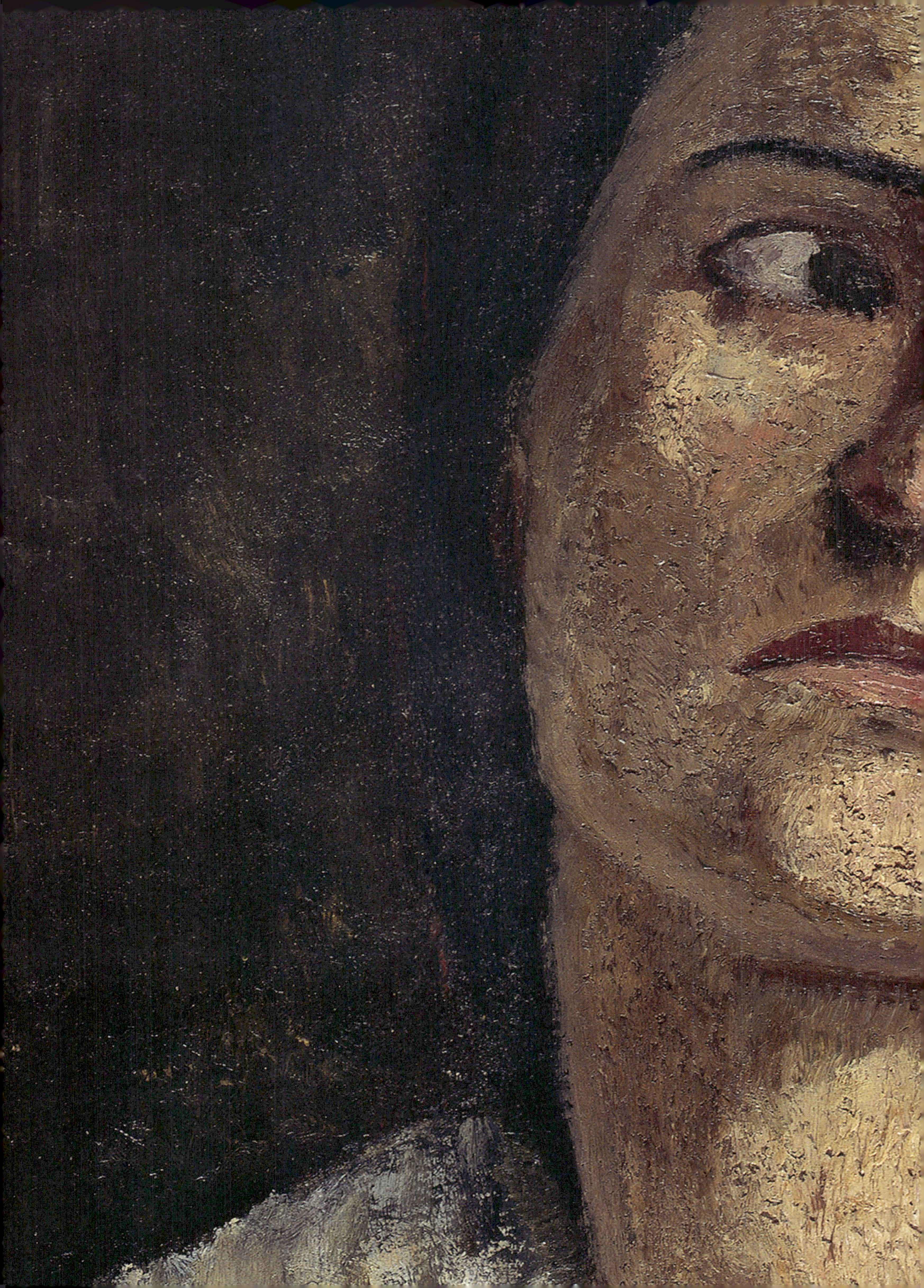

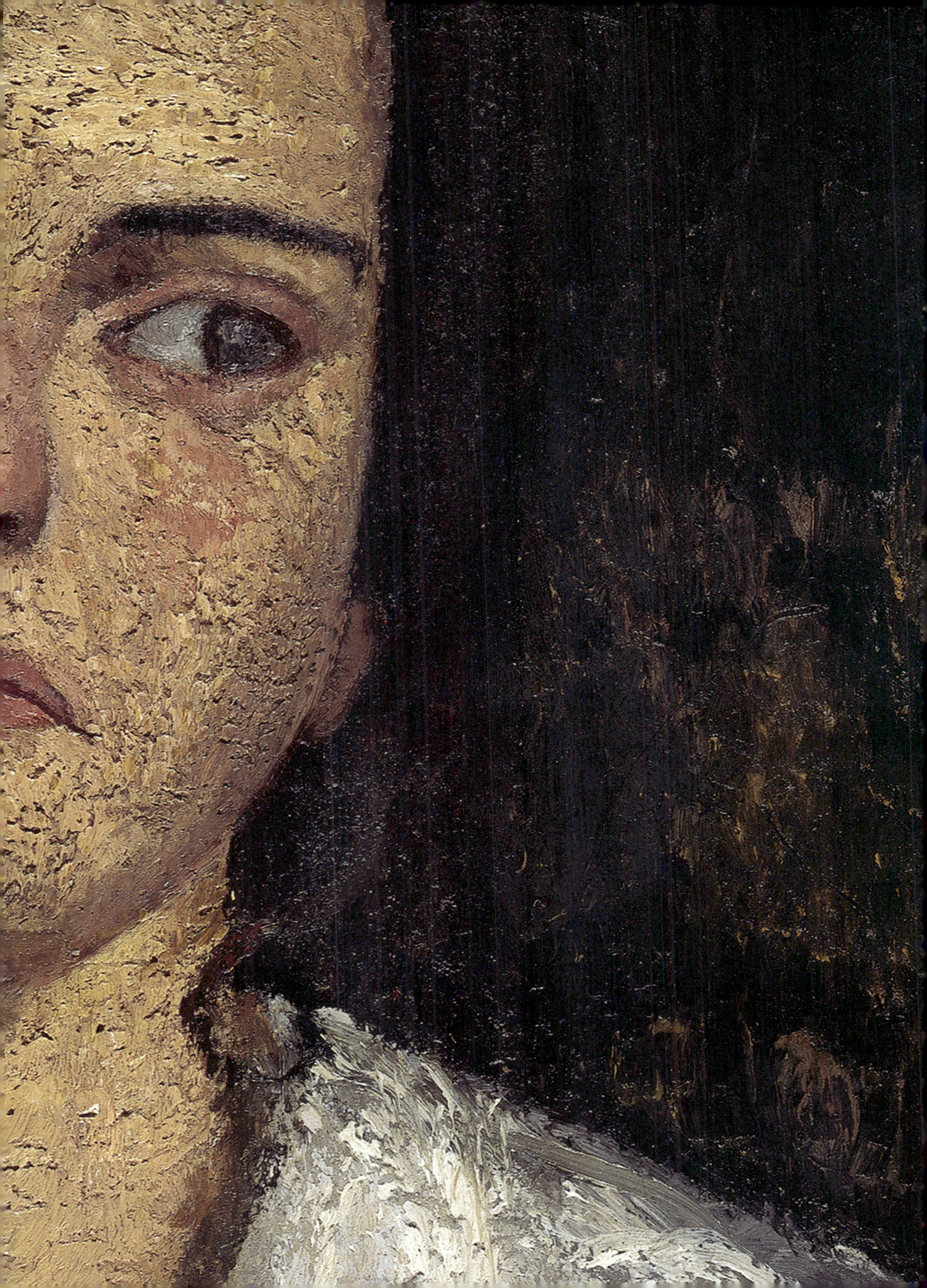

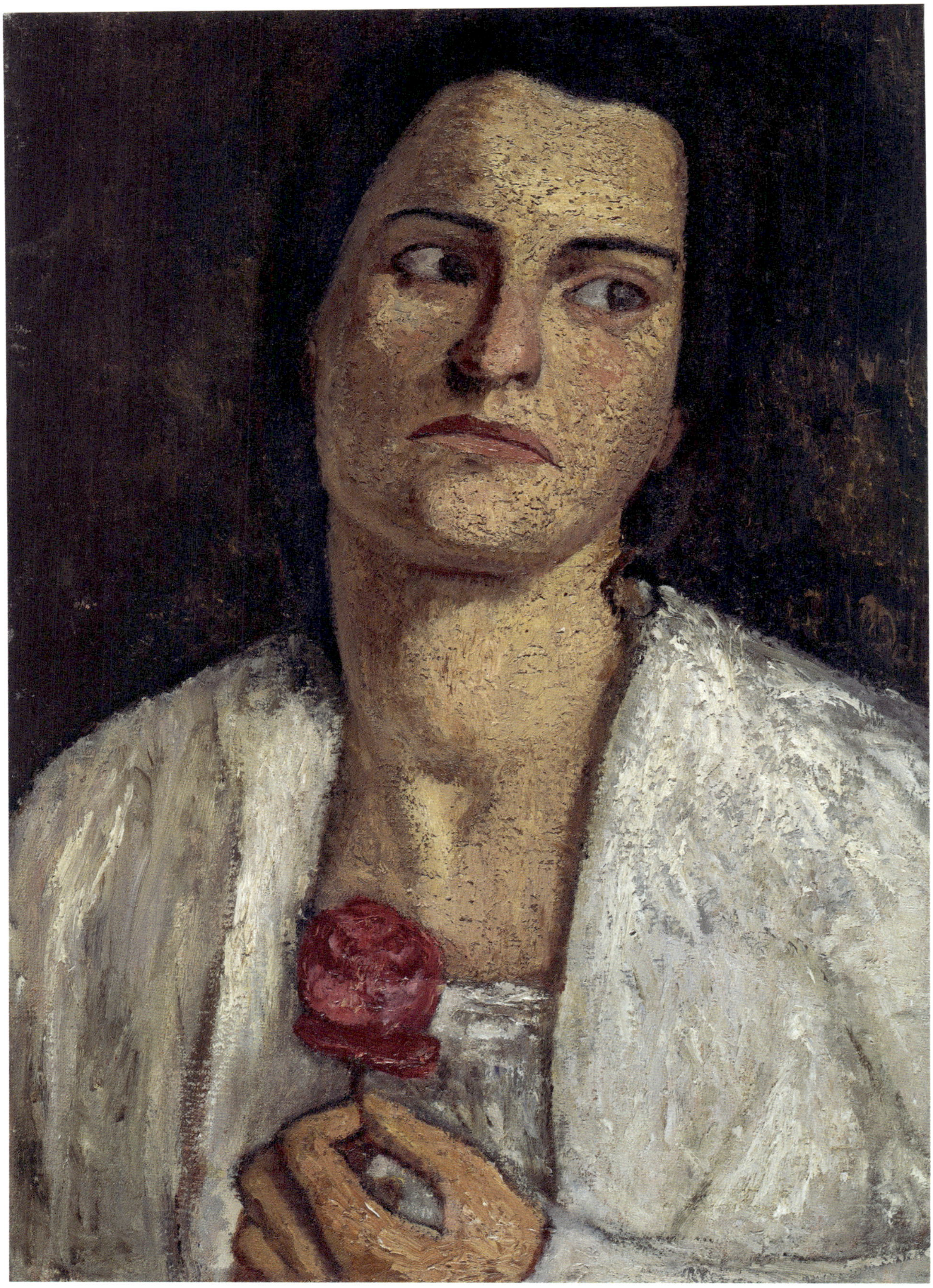

The Sculptor Clara Rilke-Westhoff, 1905

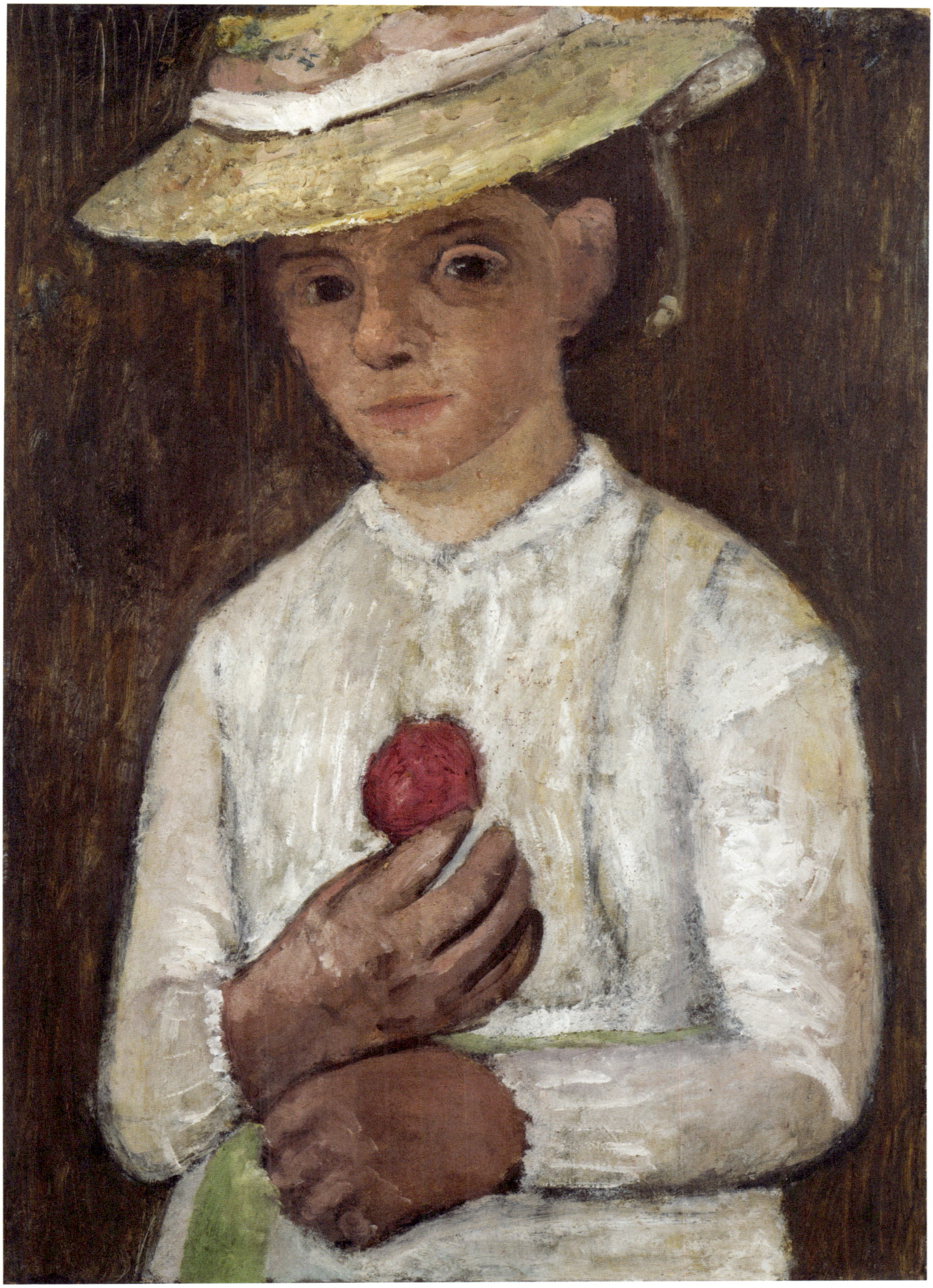

Self-Portrait with Red Rose, c. 1905

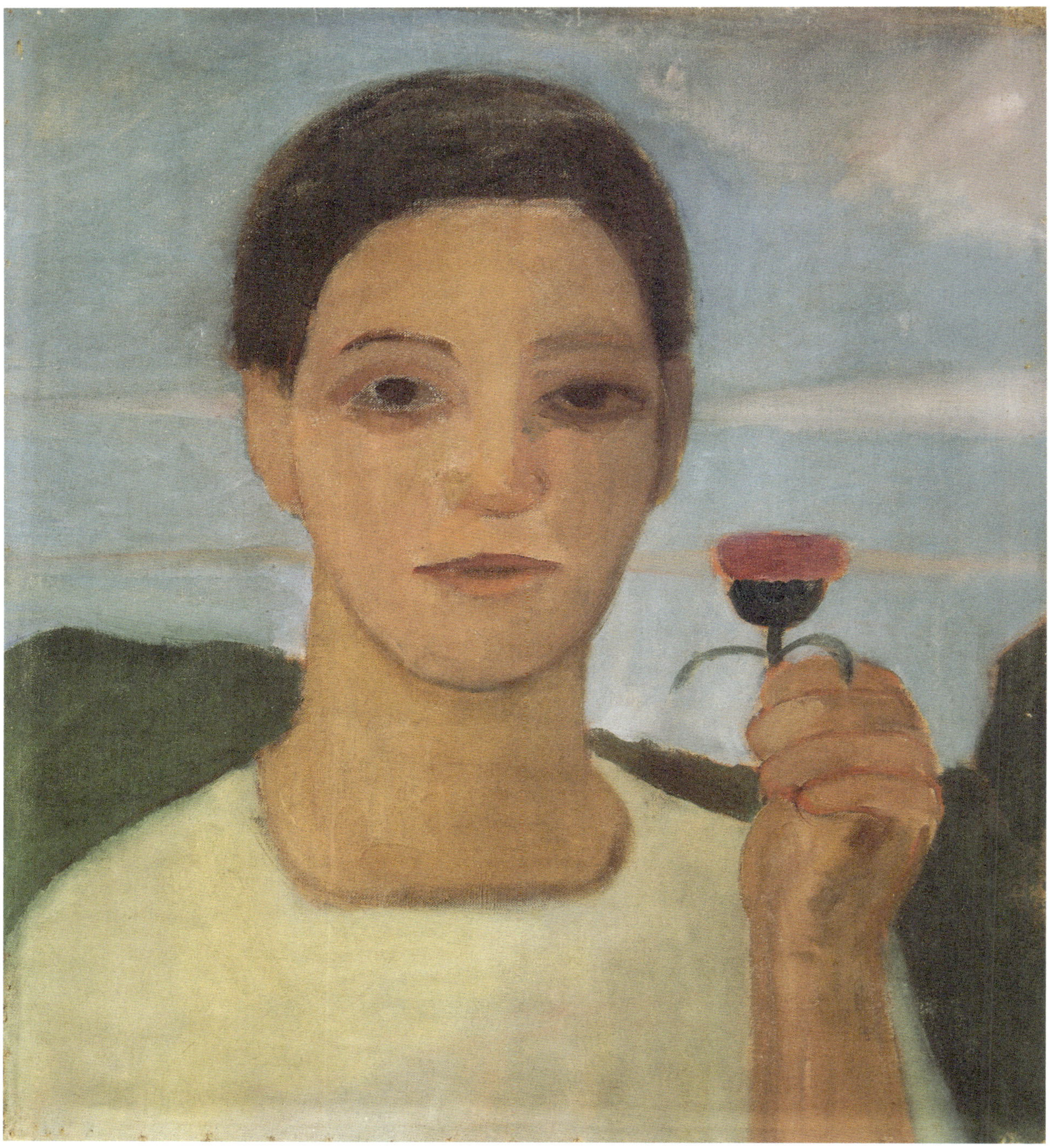

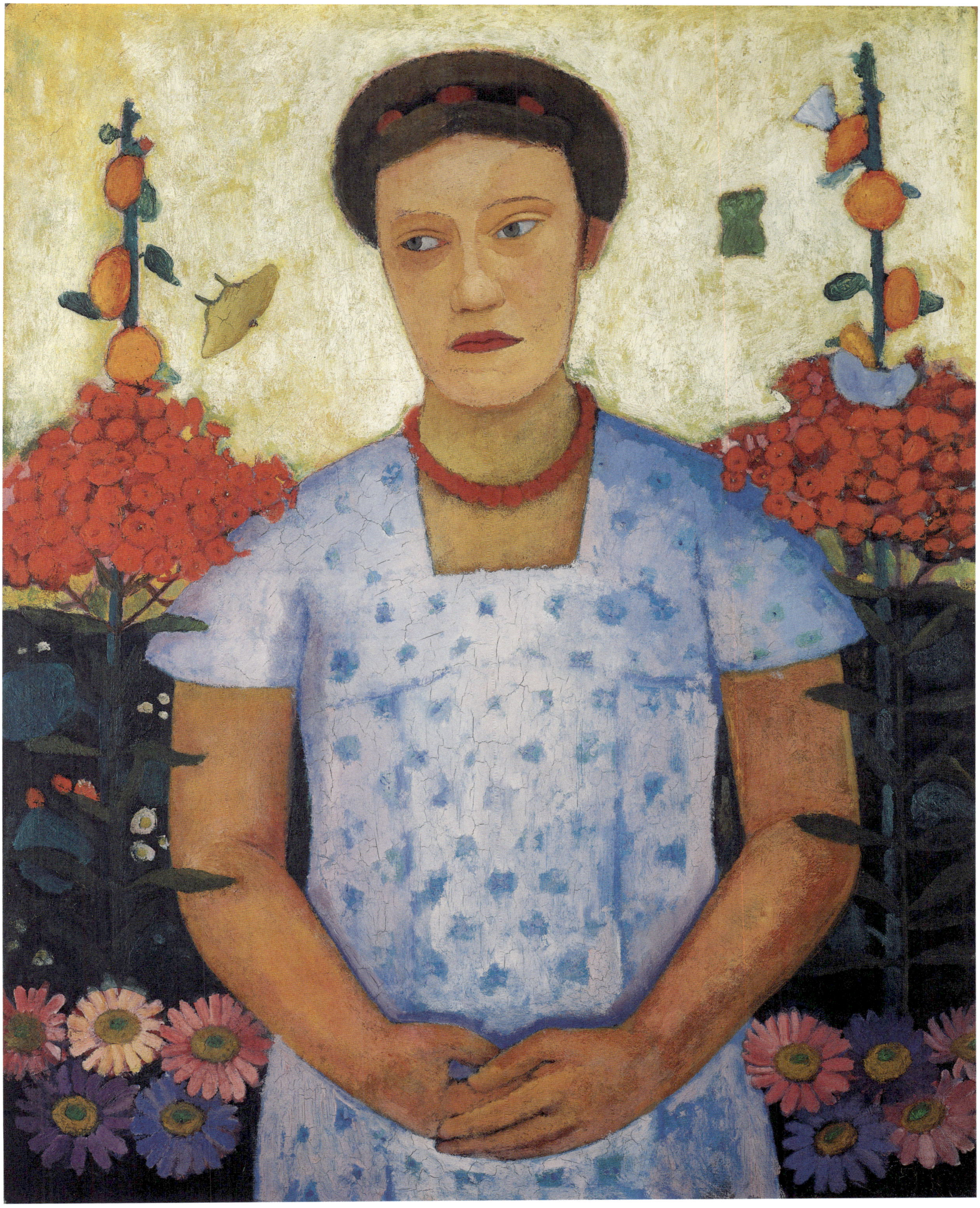

Portrait of Sister Herma with Artichoke Blossom in Raised Hand, 1906

Portrait of Lee Hoetger in front of a Floral Background, 1906

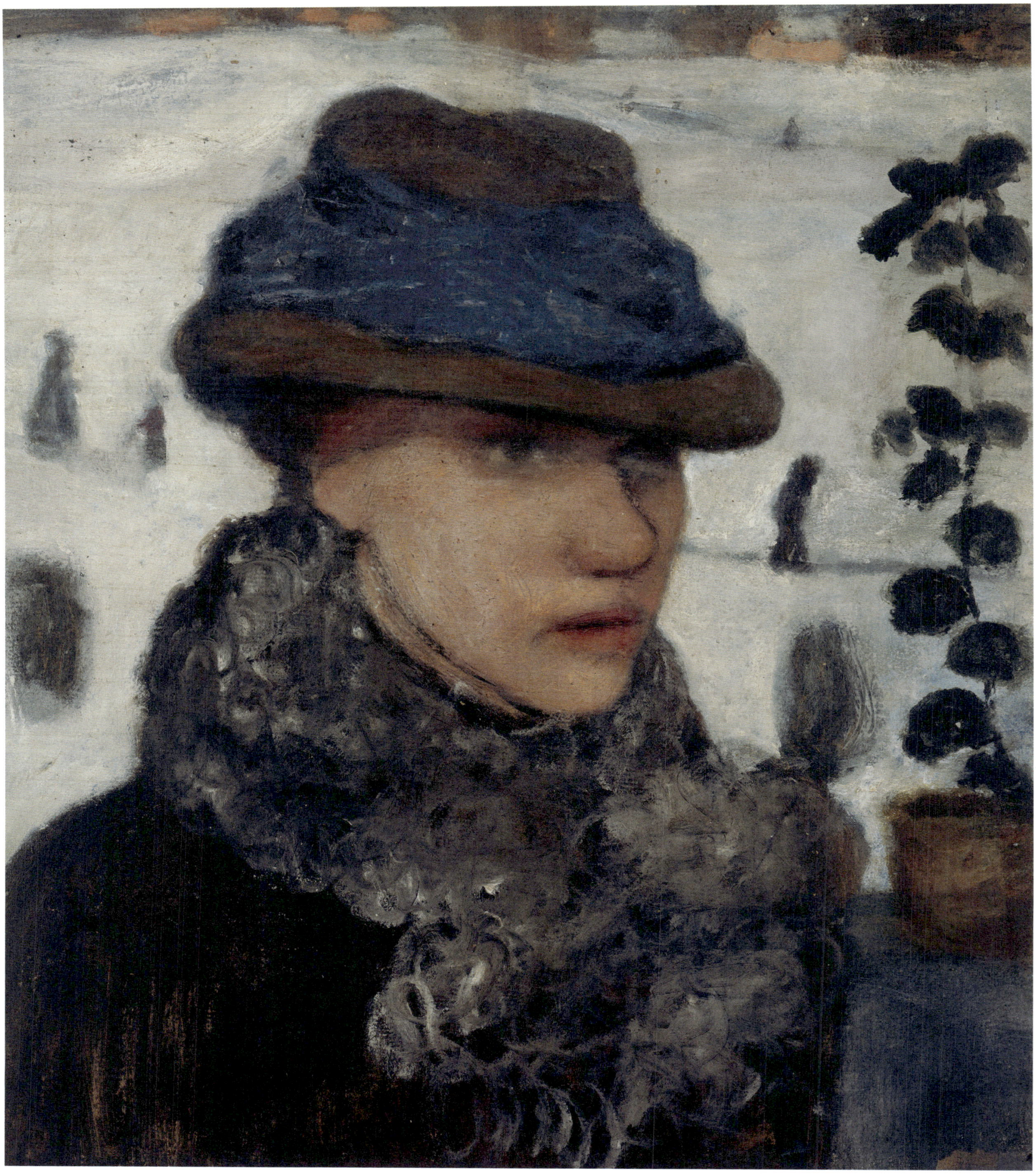

Portrait of Martha Vogeler in front of a Winter Landscape, 1906

Portrait of Rainer Maria Rilke, 1906

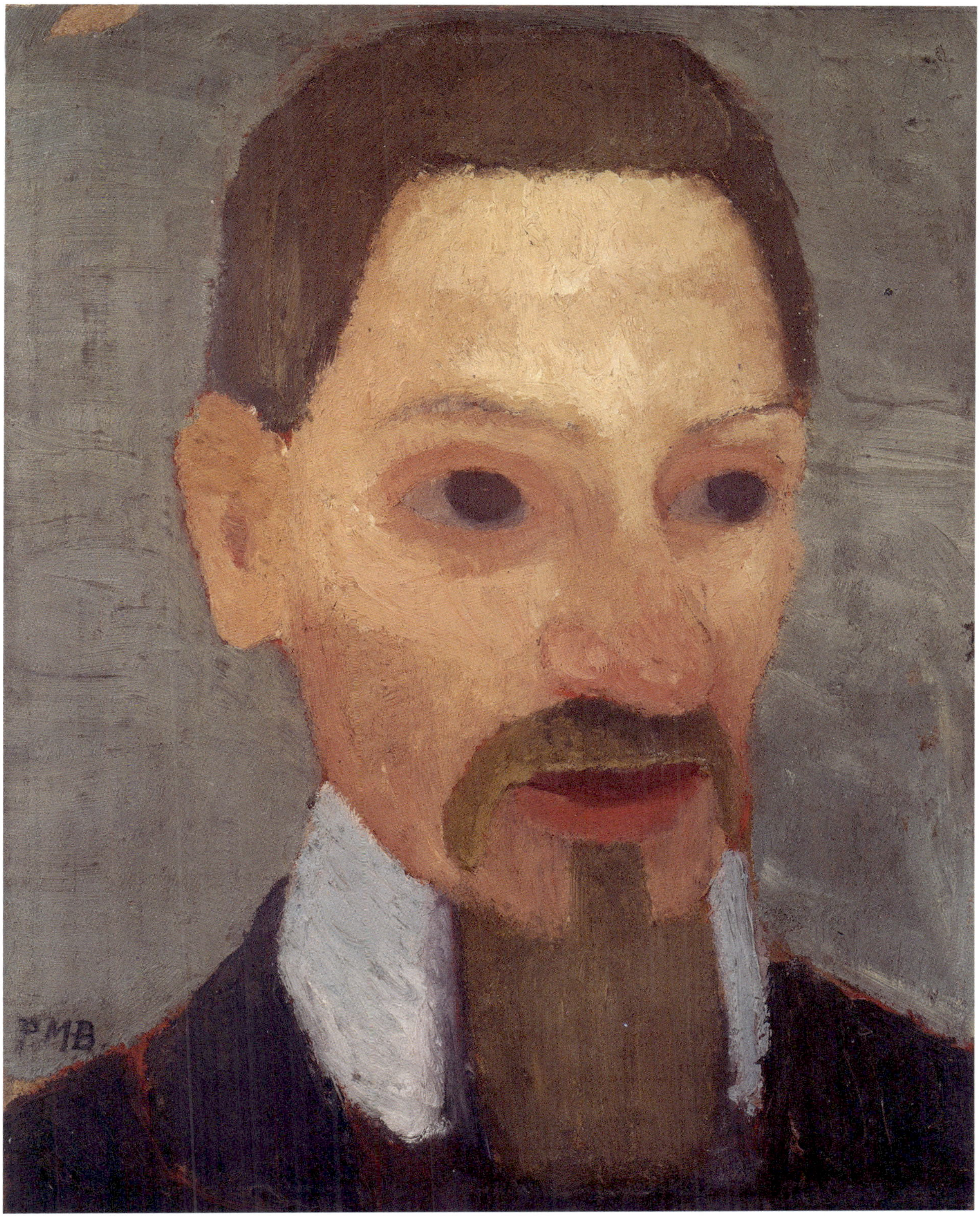
P.MB.

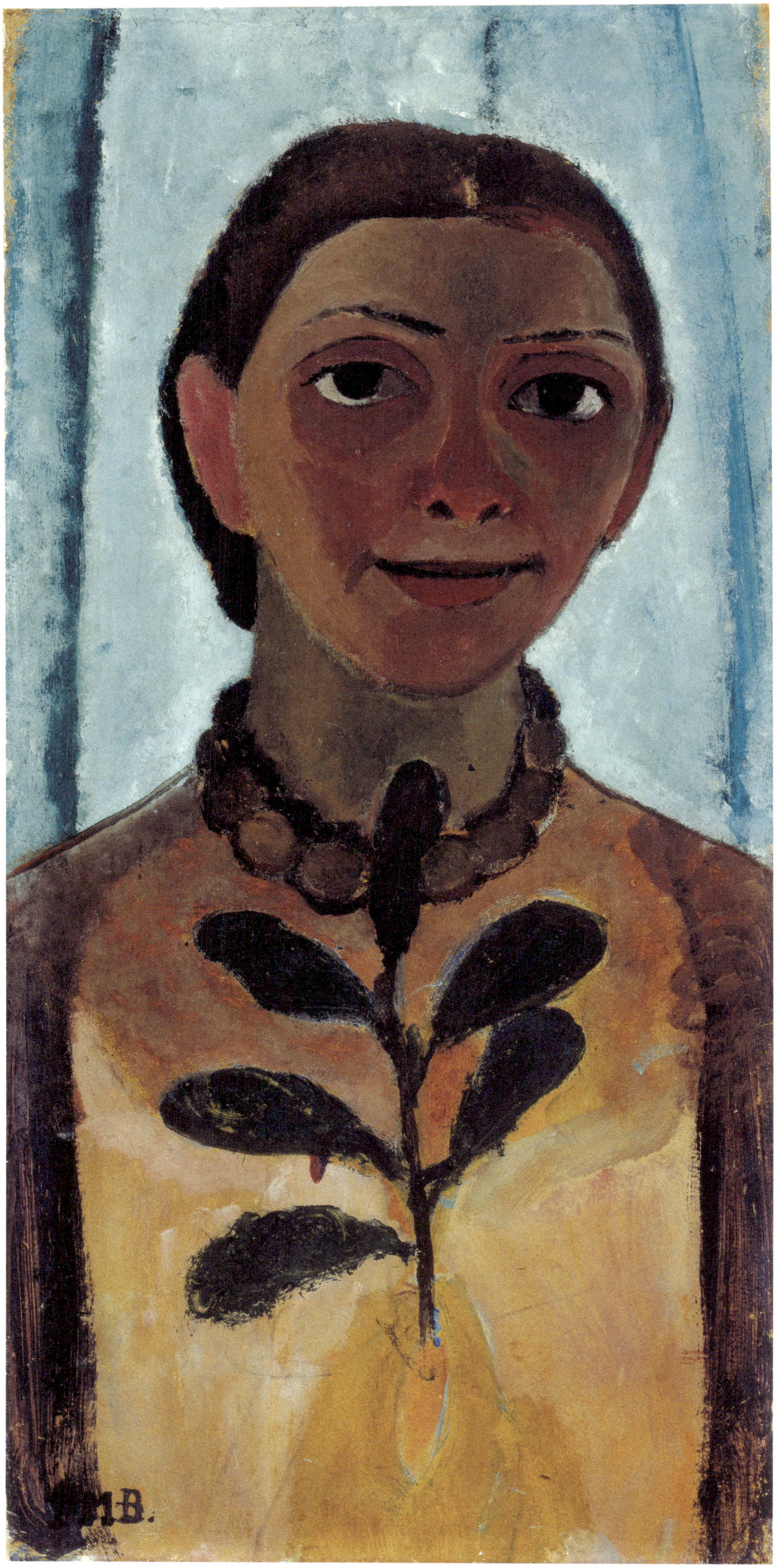

5

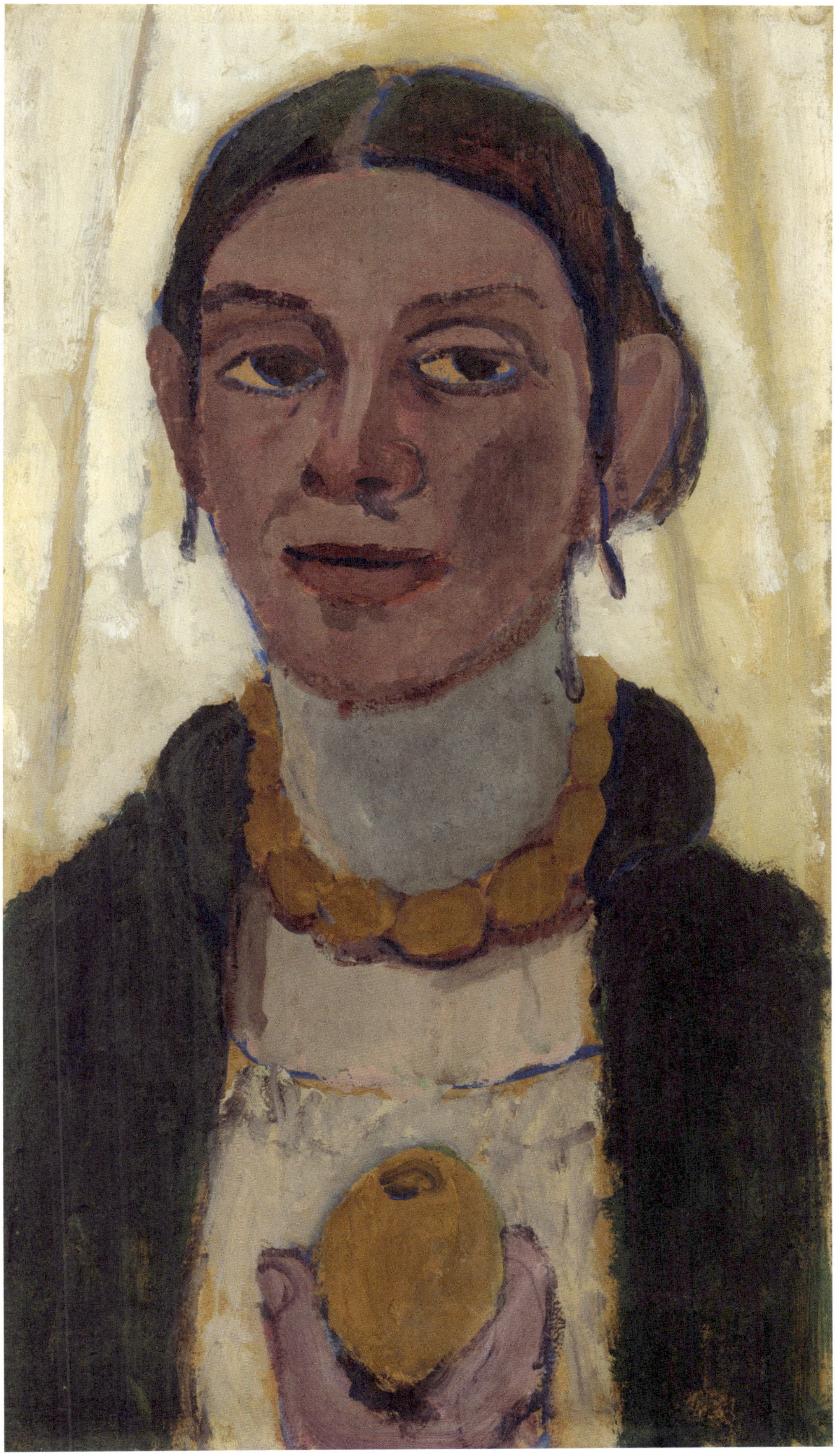

Self-Portrait with Sprig of Camellias, 1906/07

Self-Portrait with Lemon, 1906/07

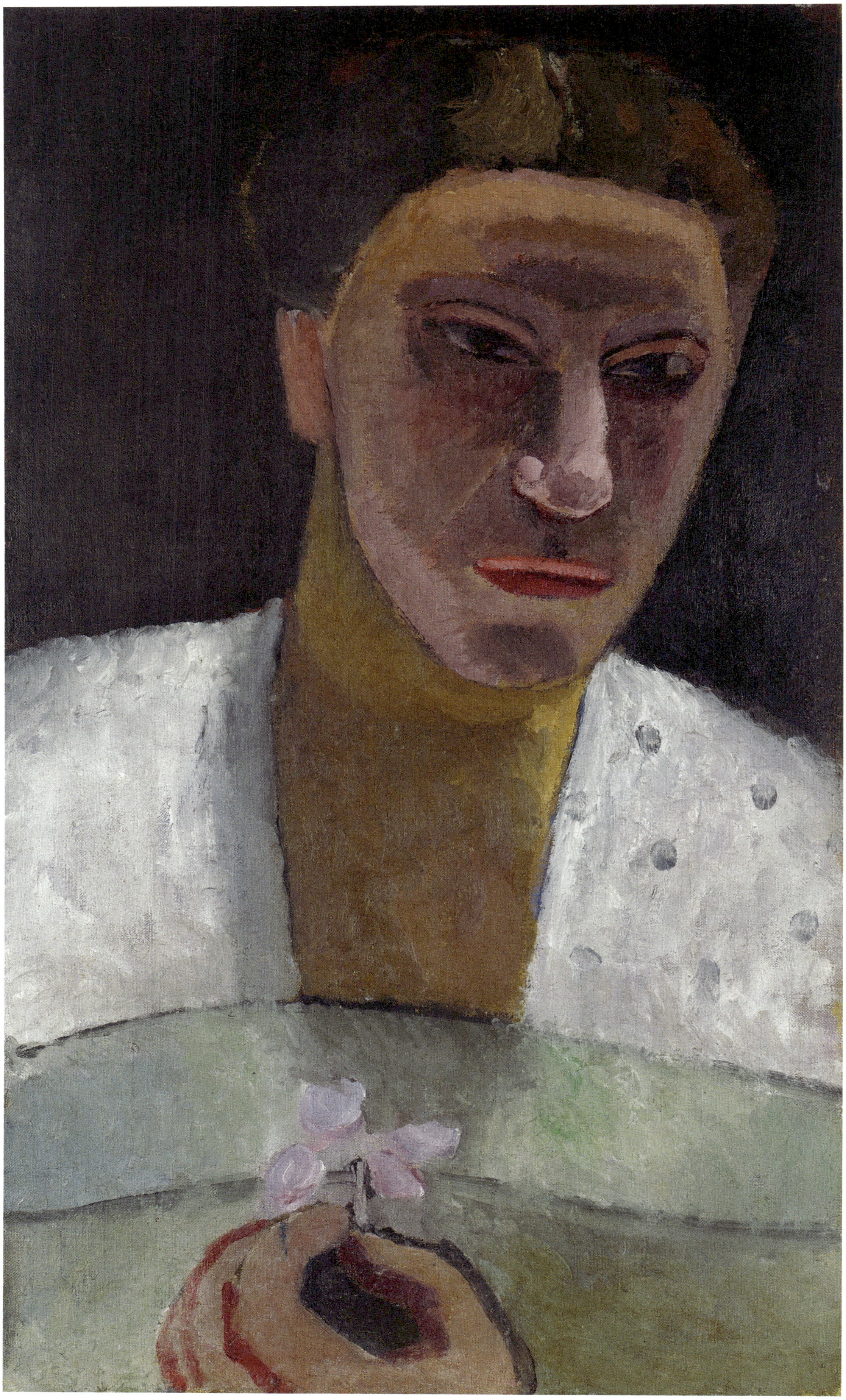

Bust Portrait of Lee Hoetger with Flower, August 1906

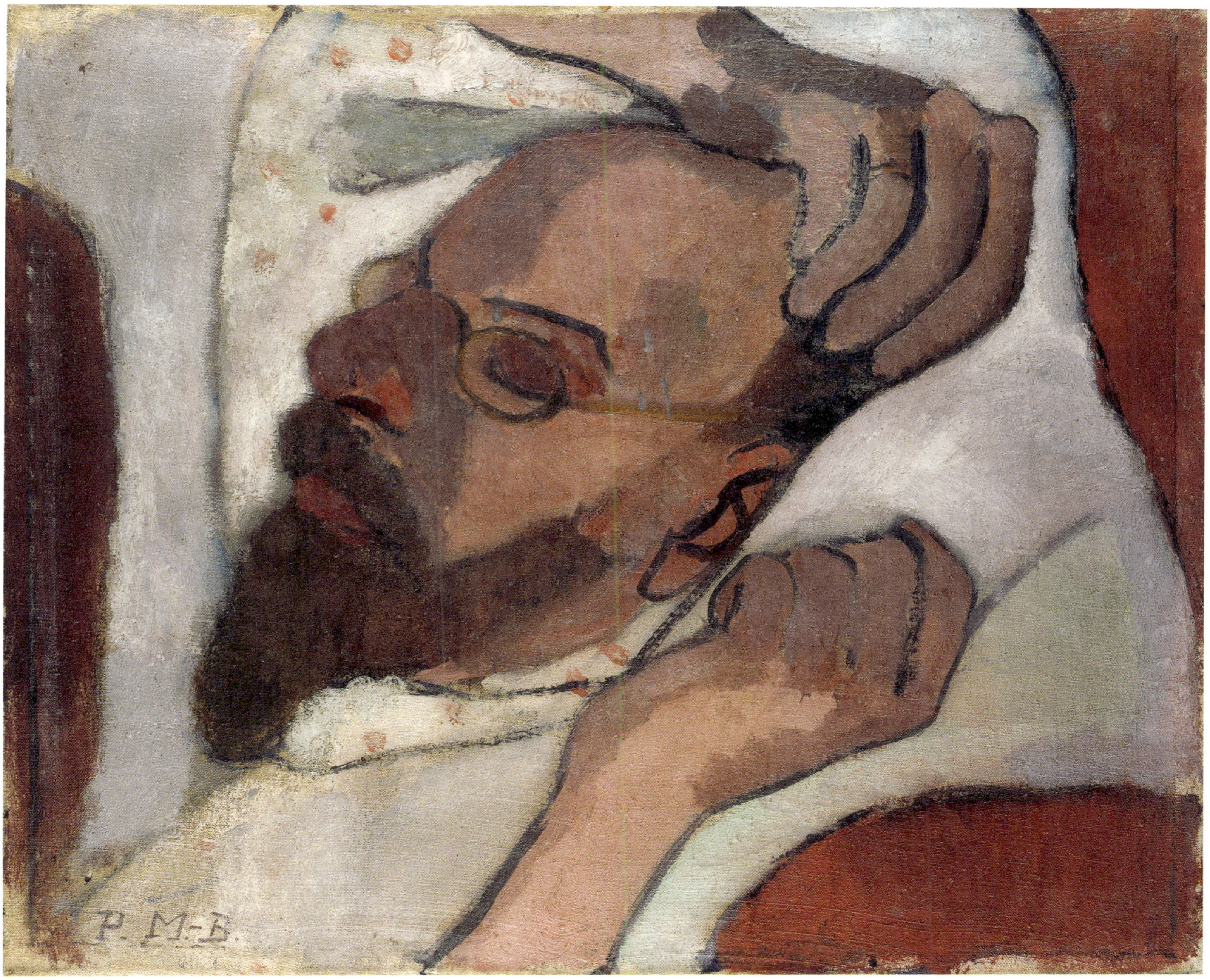

Otto Modersohn Sleeping, 1907

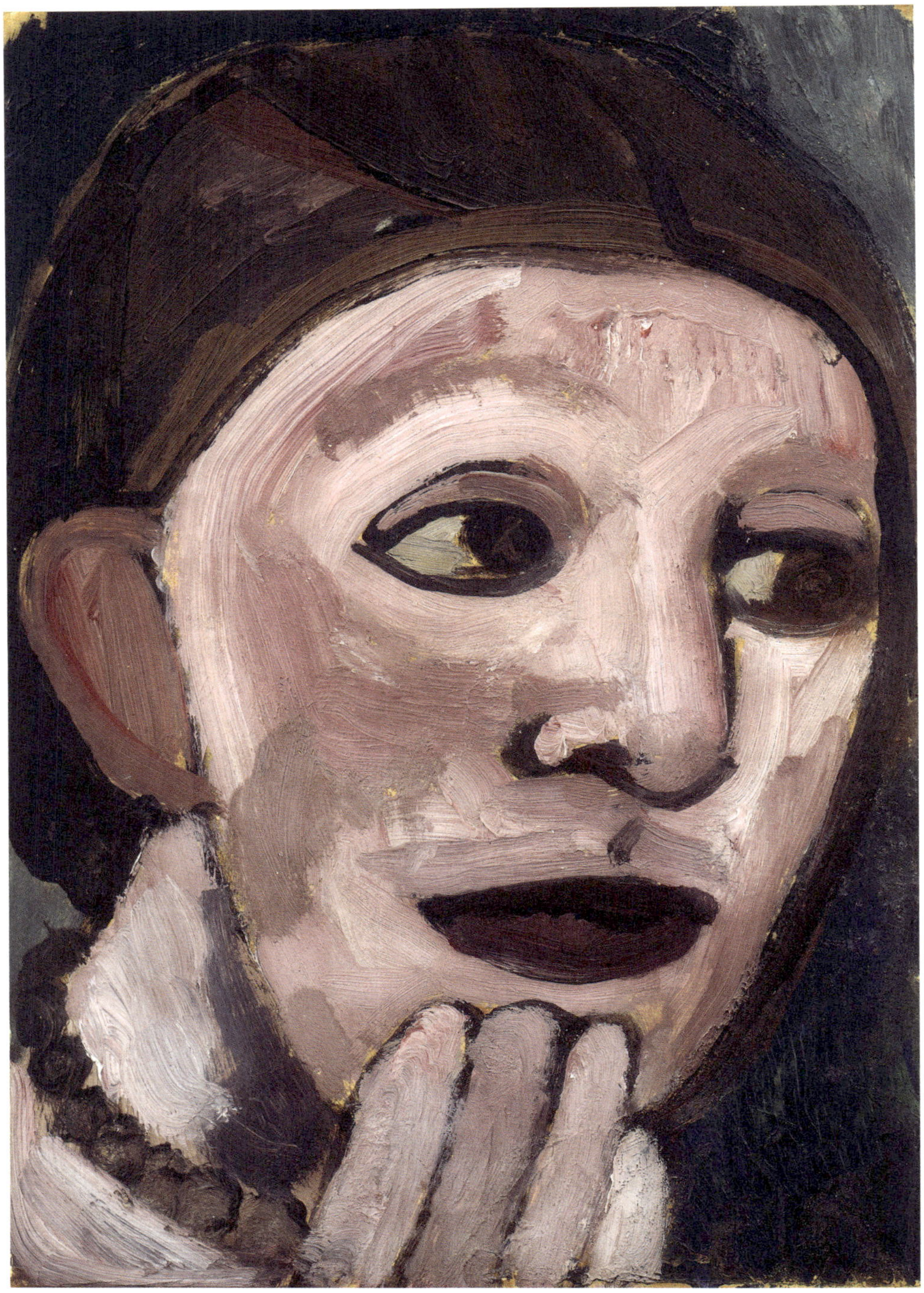

Self-Portrait Half-Turned to the Right, Her Hand on Her Chin, summer, 1906

Old Poorhouse Woman in the Garden with Glass Ball and Poppies, 1907

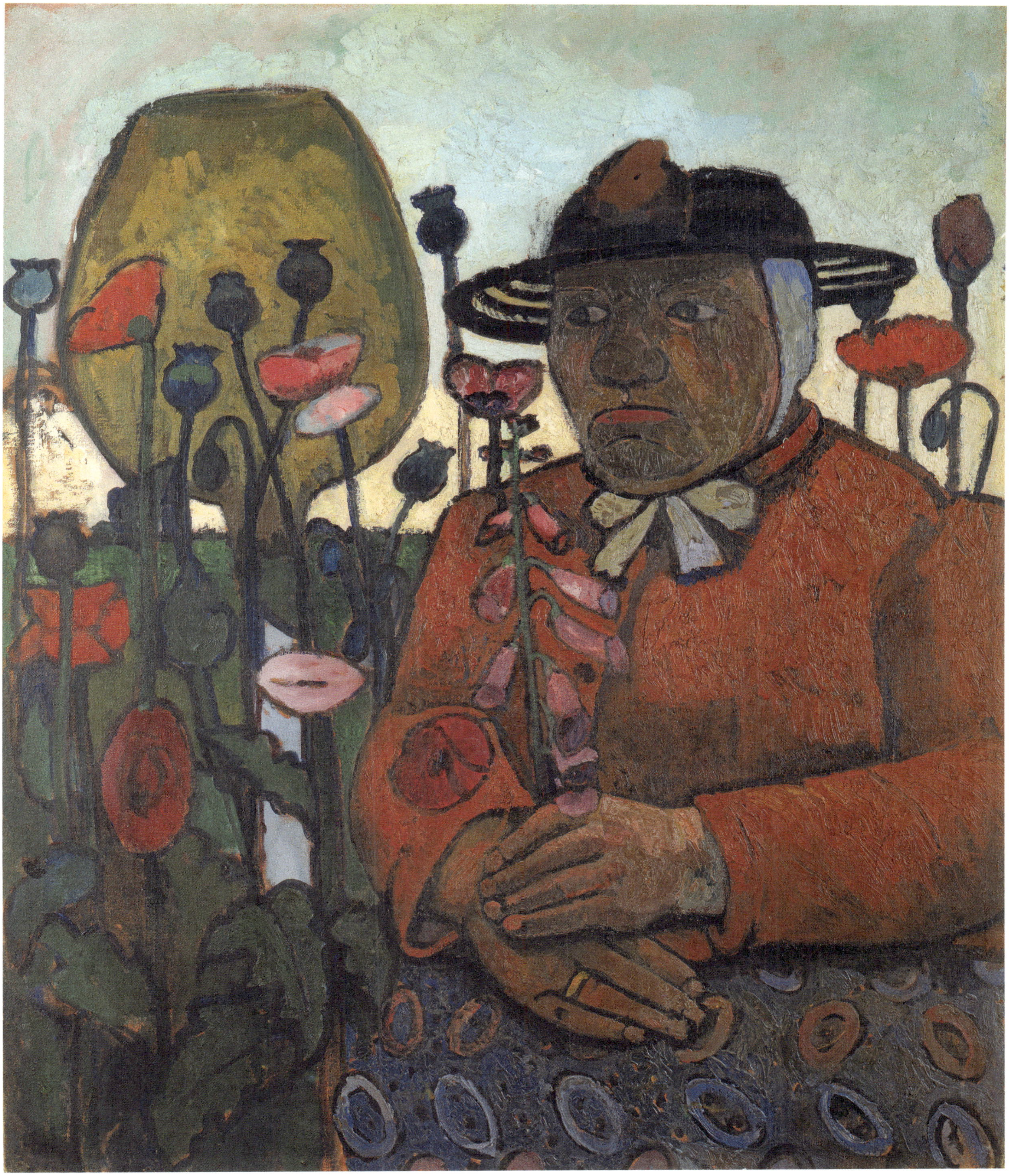

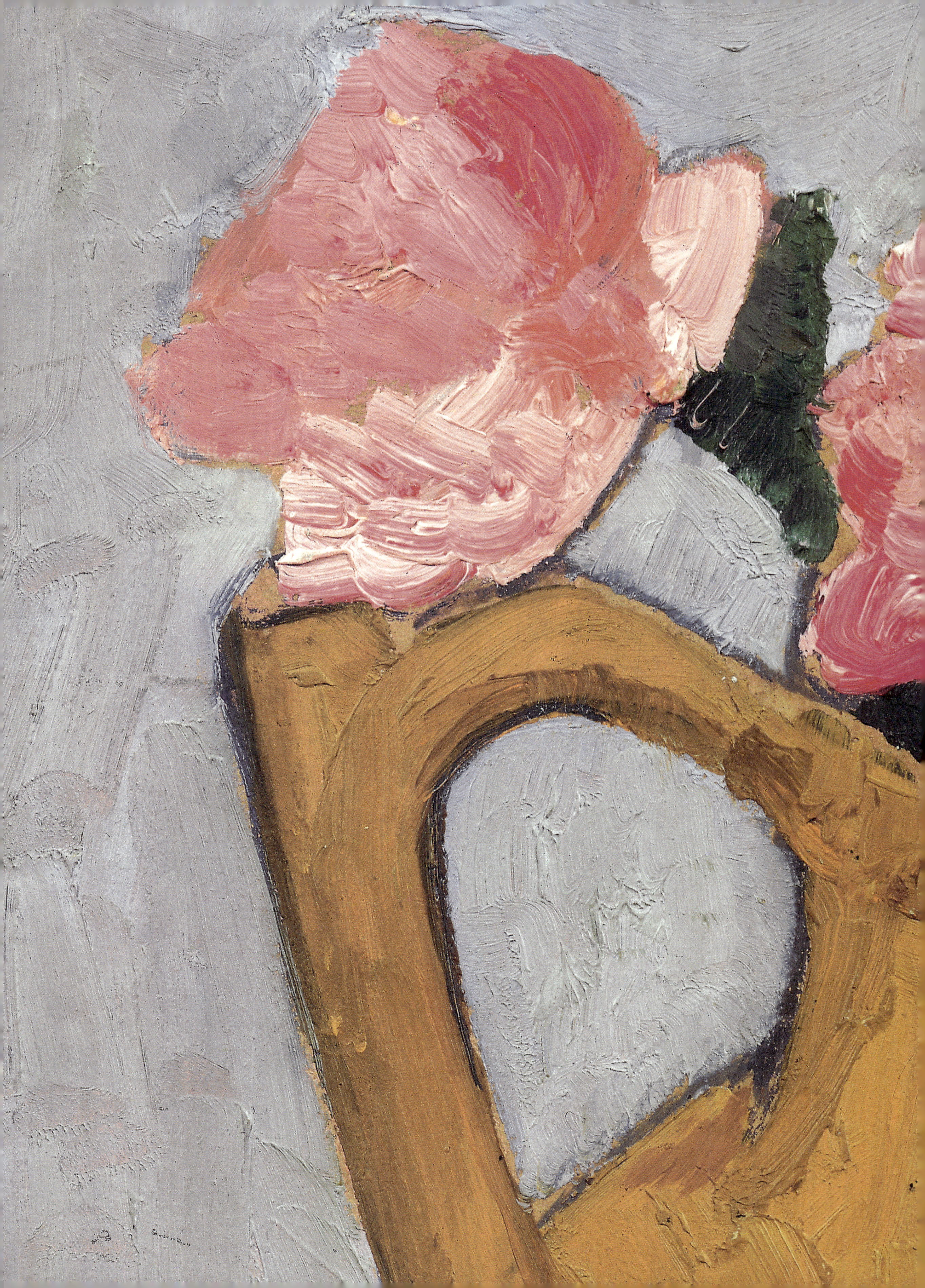

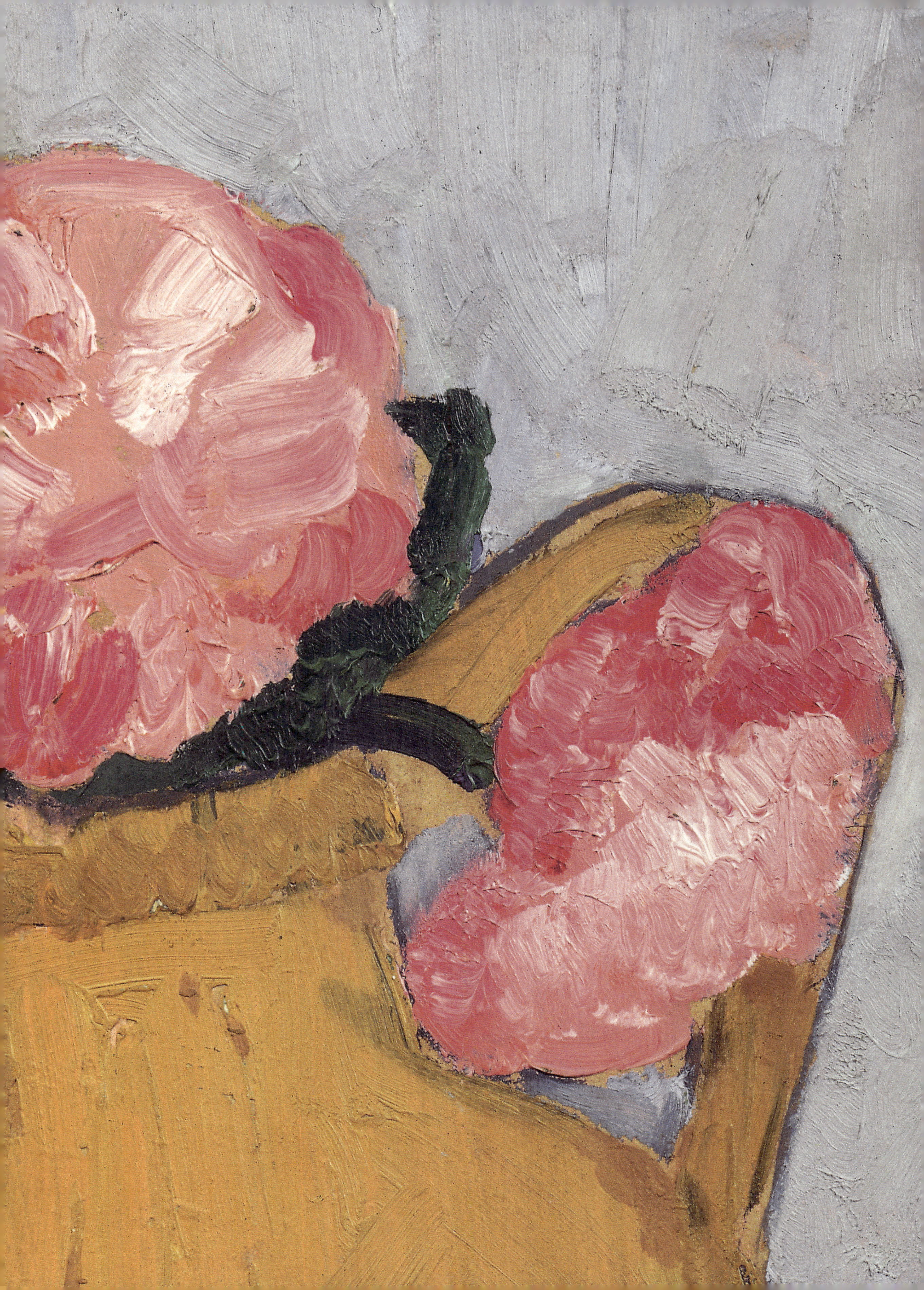

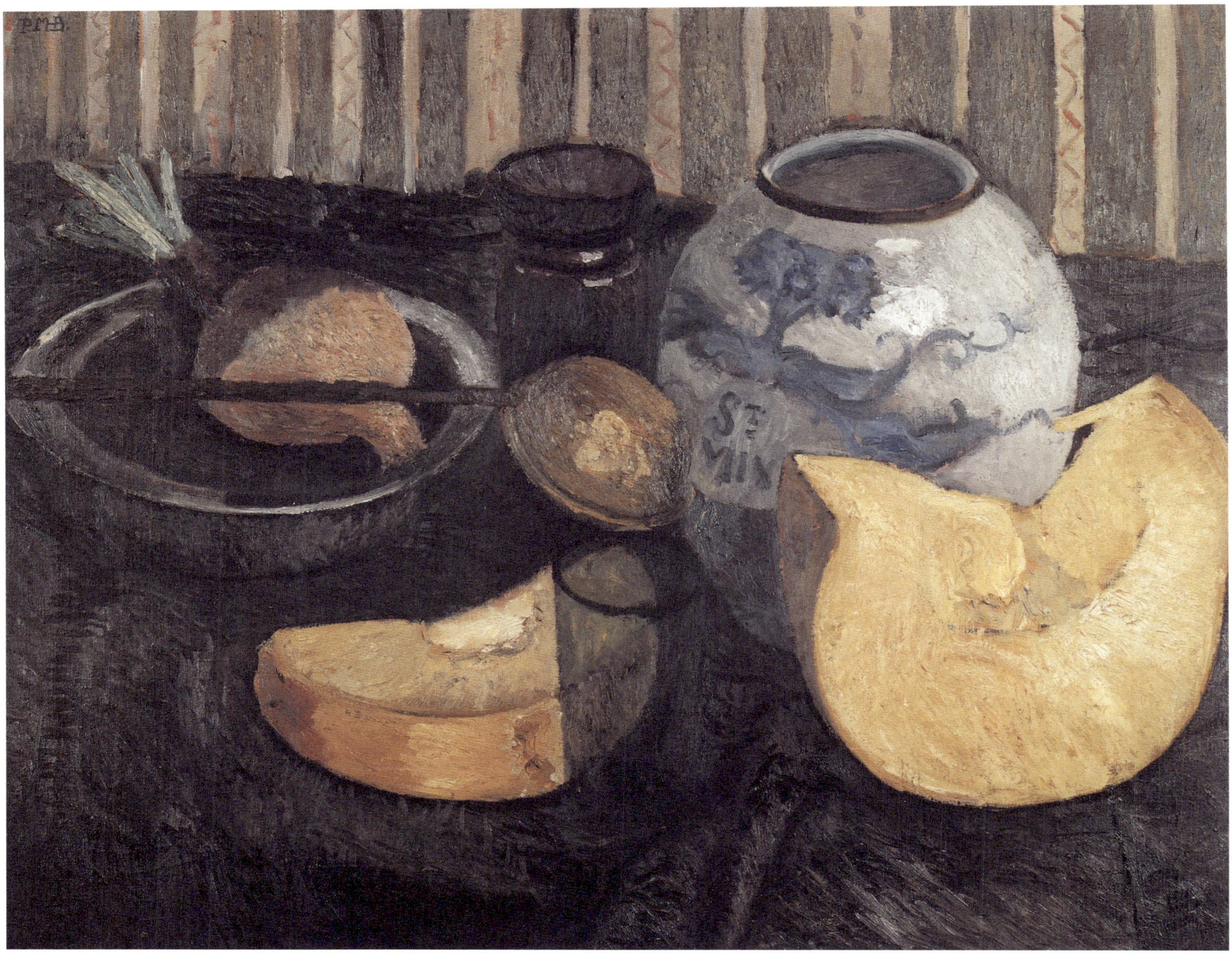

Still Life with Pumpkin and Ginger Pot, 1905

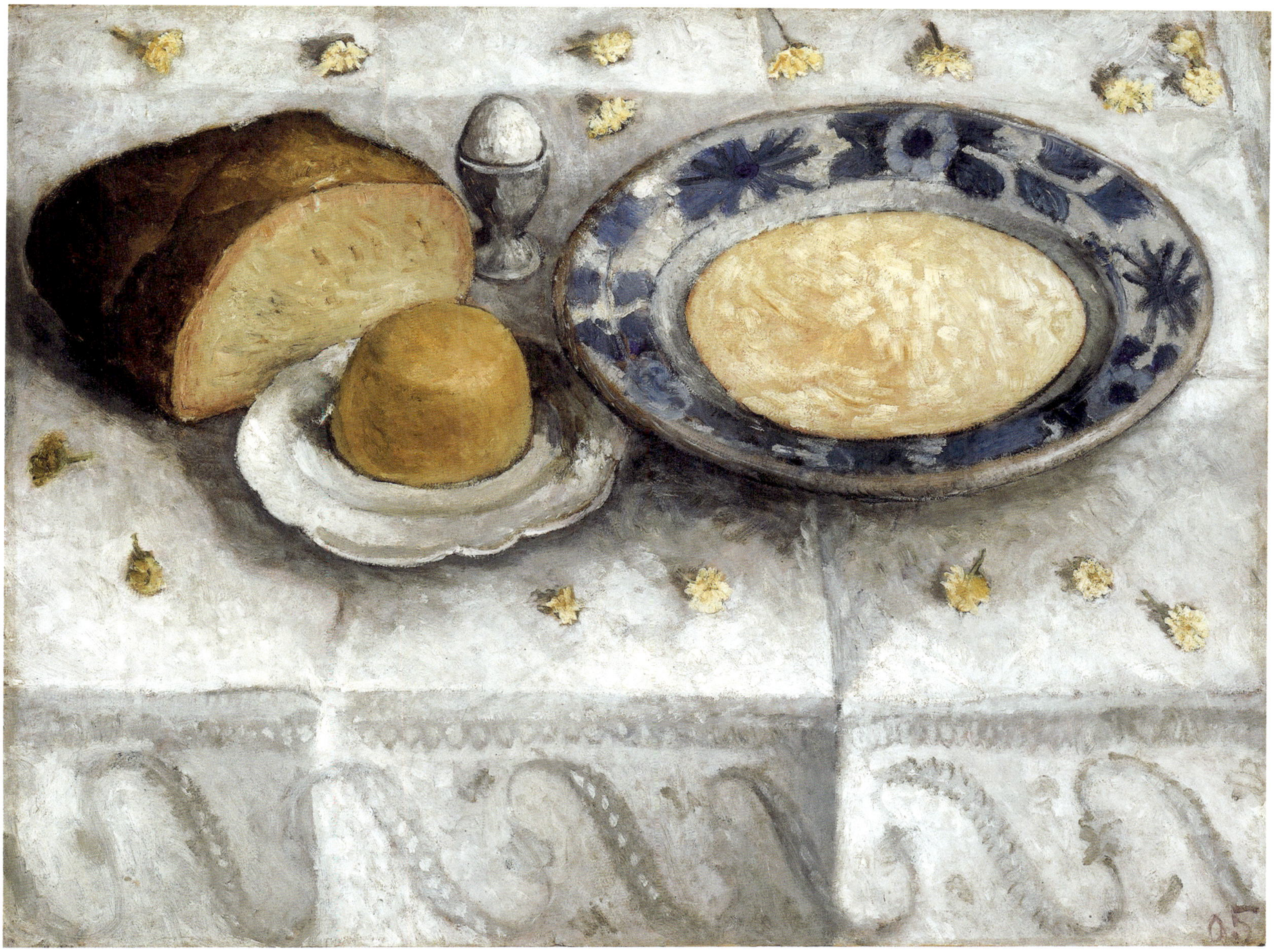

Still Life with Milk Bowl, 1905

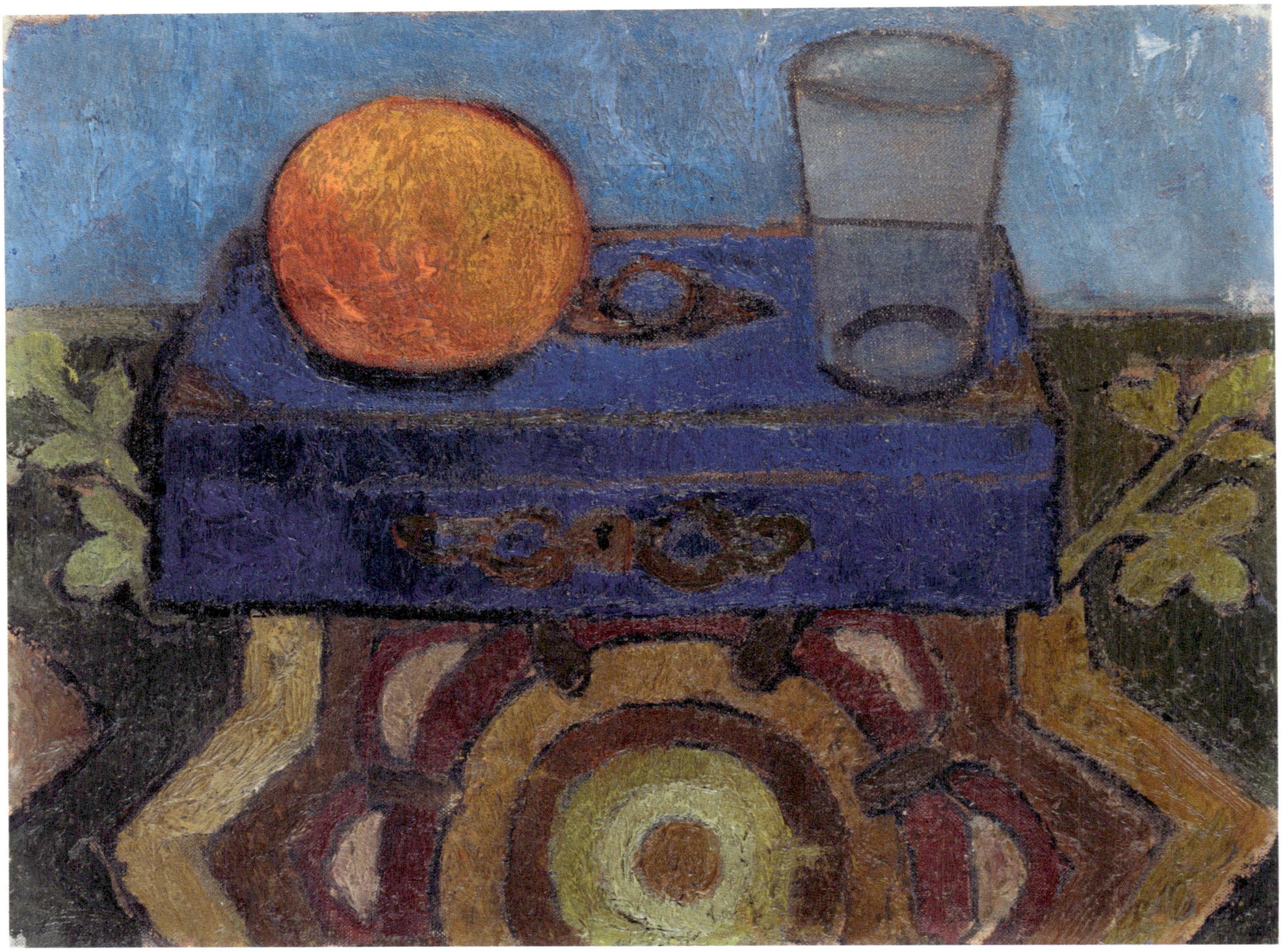

Still Life with Blue Box, 1907

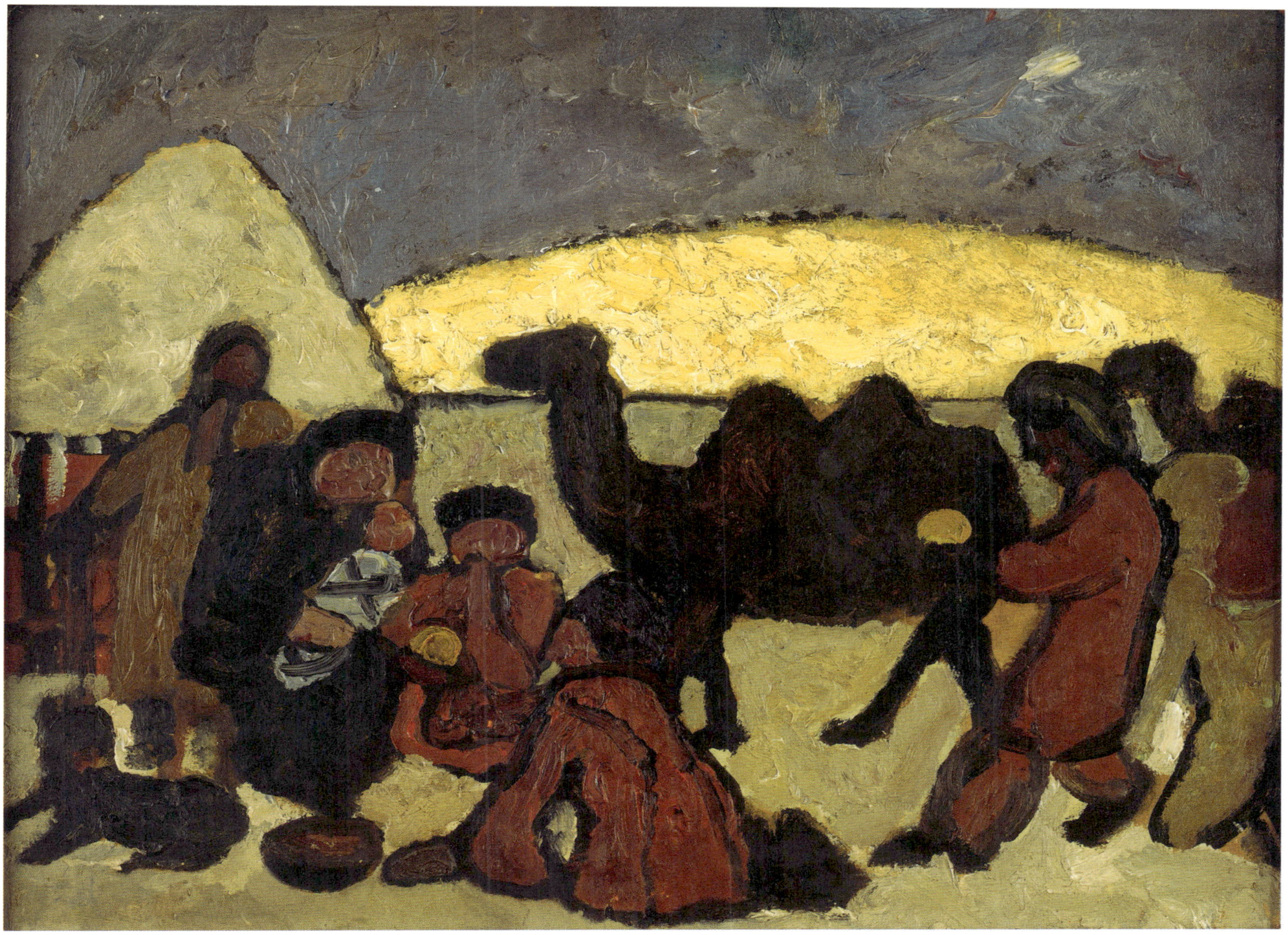

Adoration of the Magi, 1907

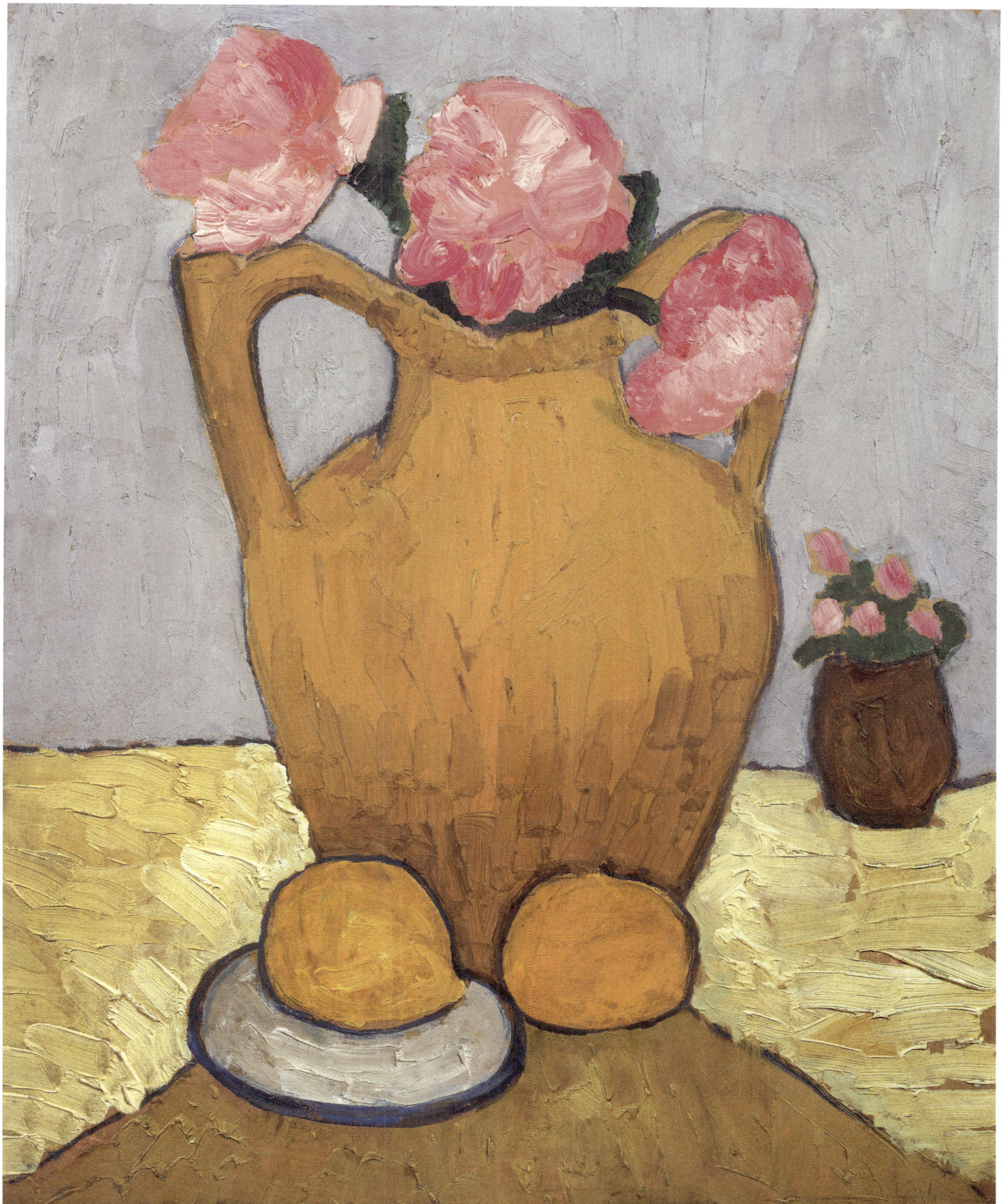

Still Life with Clay Jug, Peonies and Oranges, 1906

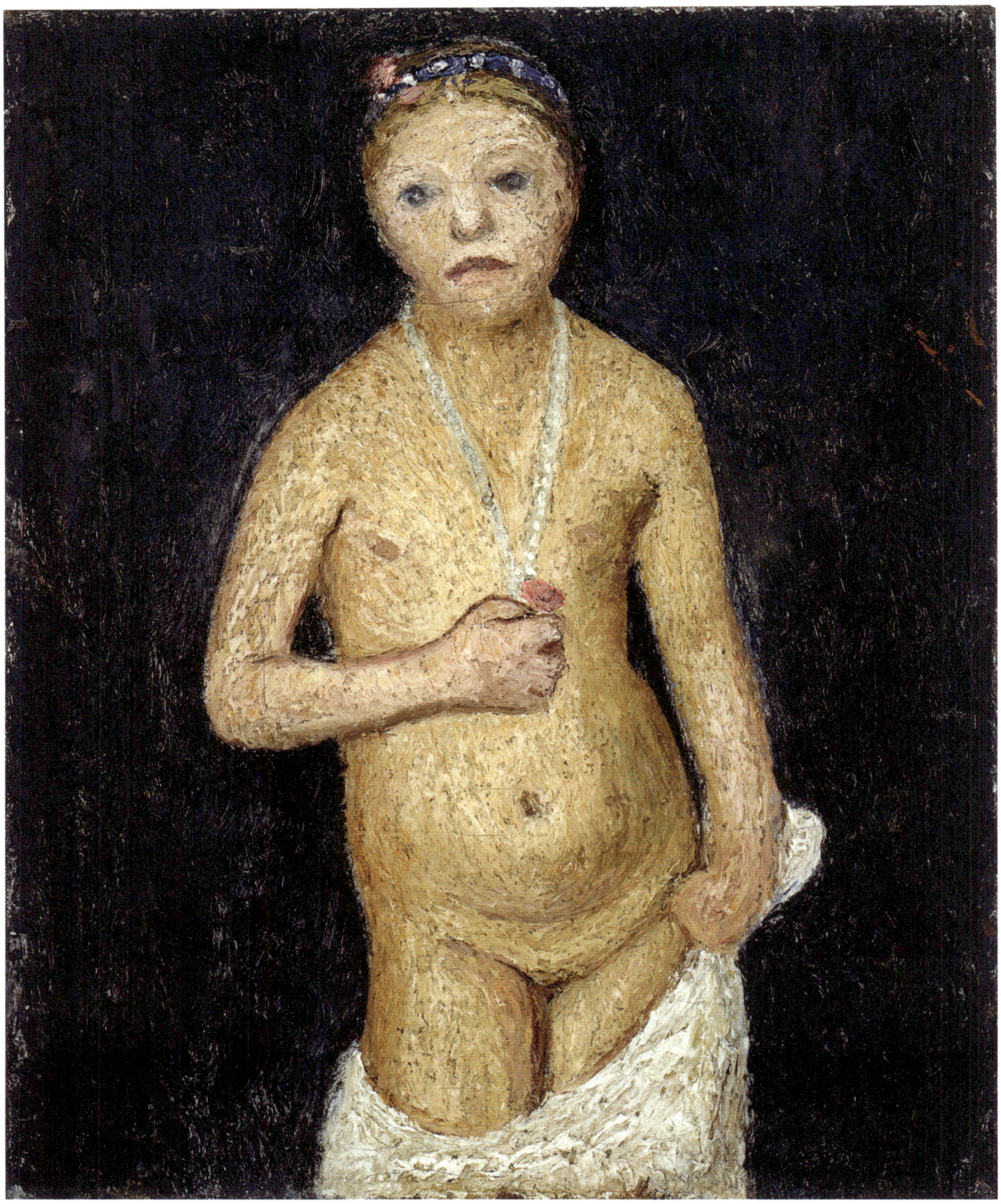

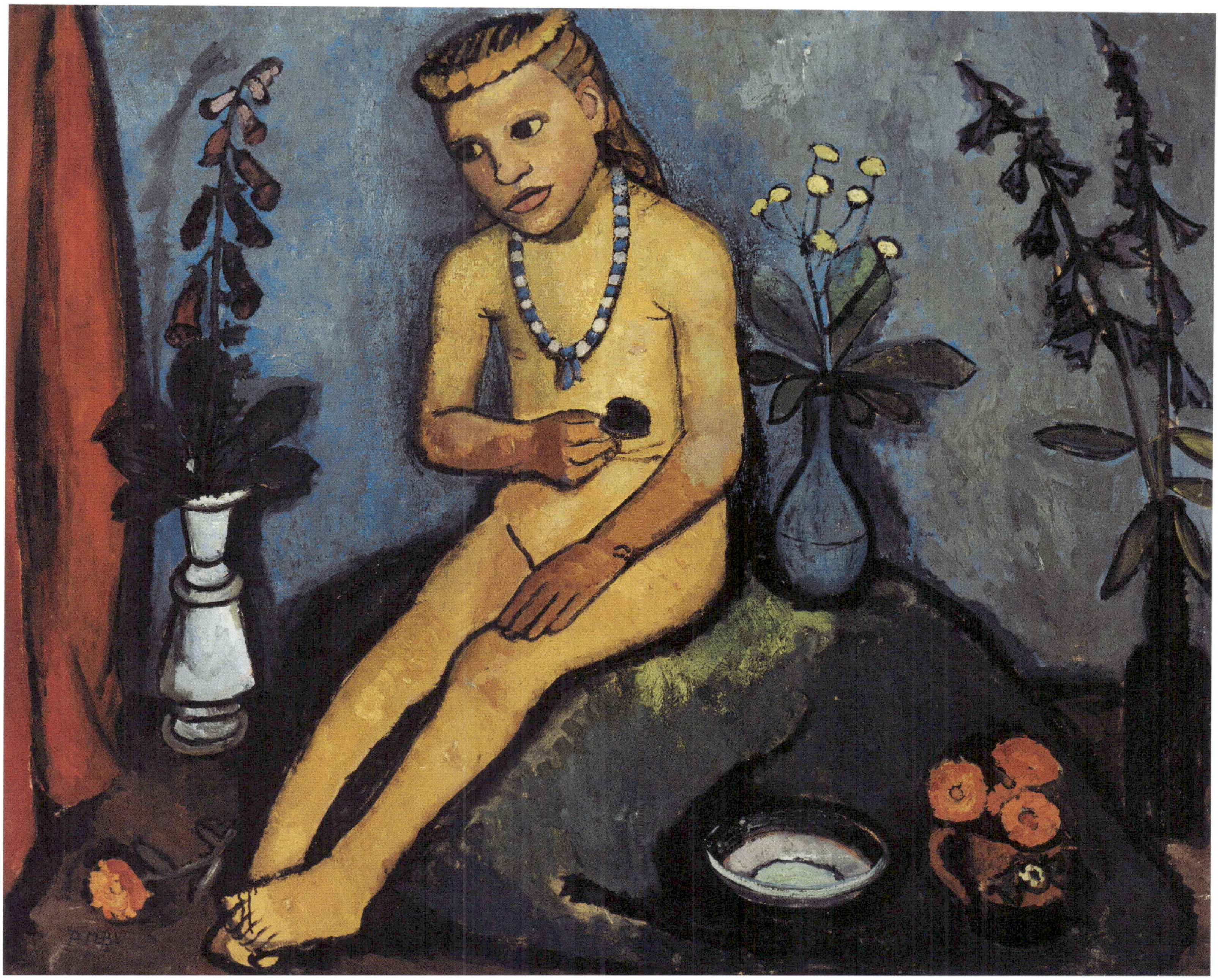

Small Standing Girl Nude with Necklace and Rose, 1906

Nude Girl with Flower Vases, 1907

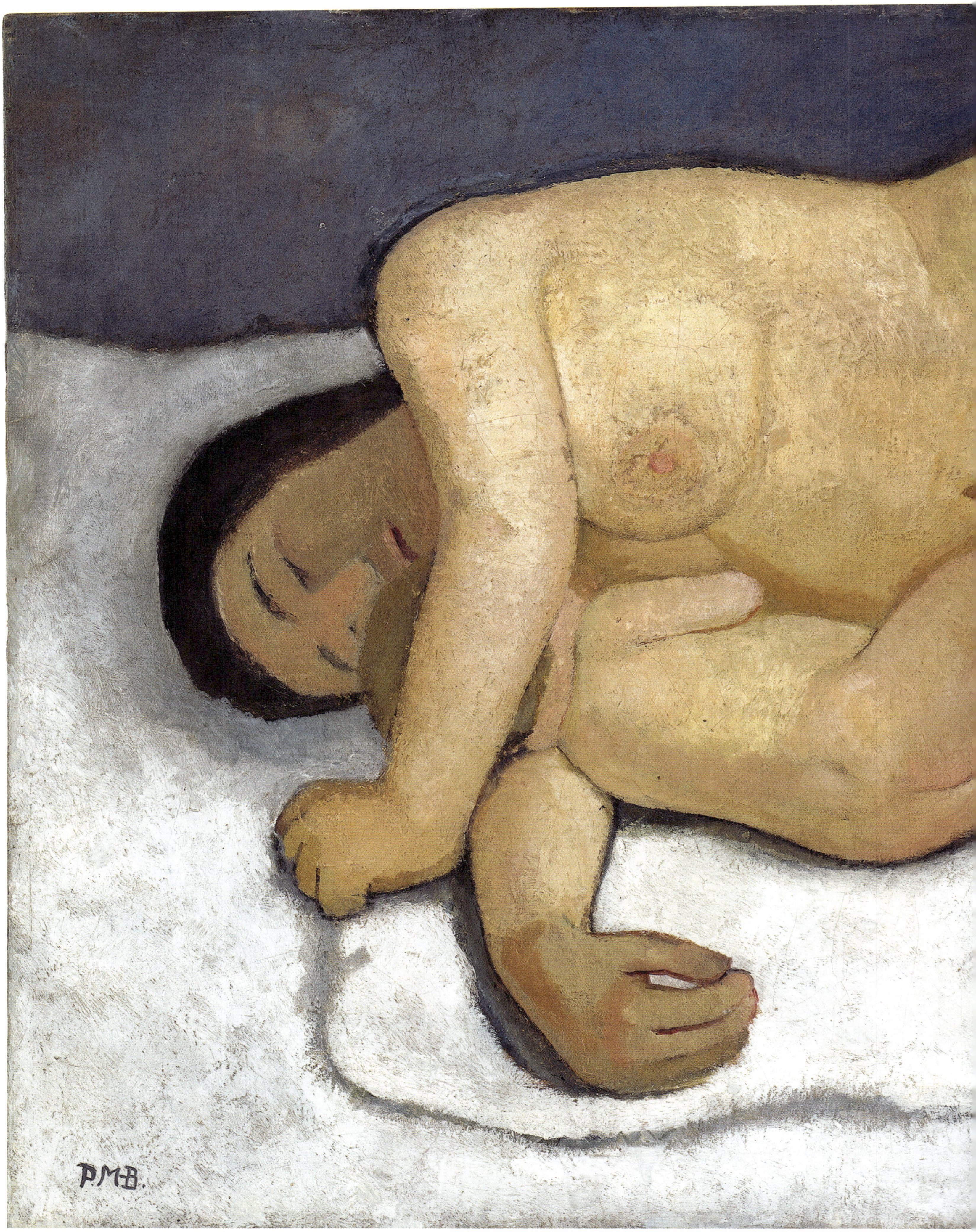

Reclining Mother with Child II, summer, 1906

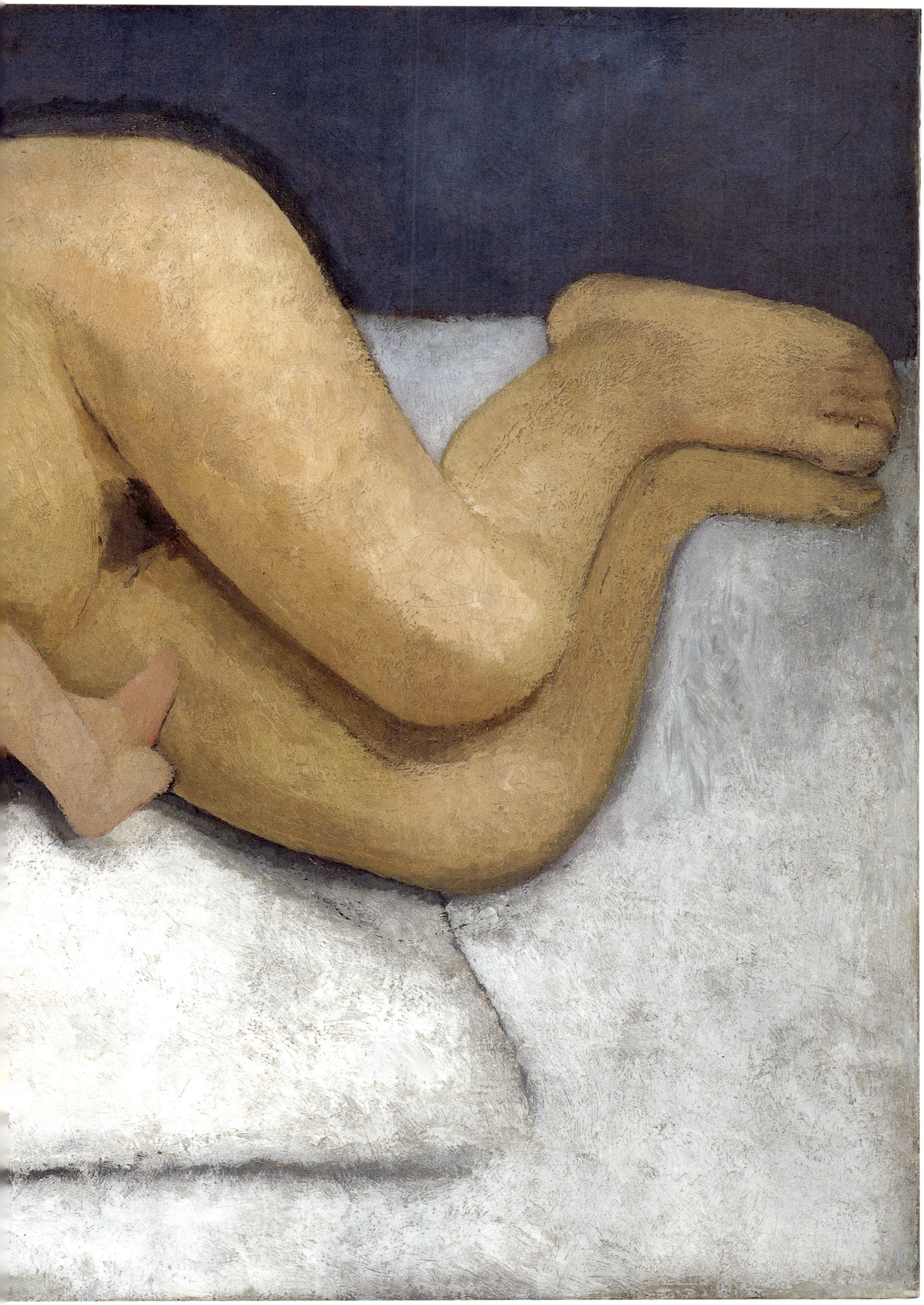

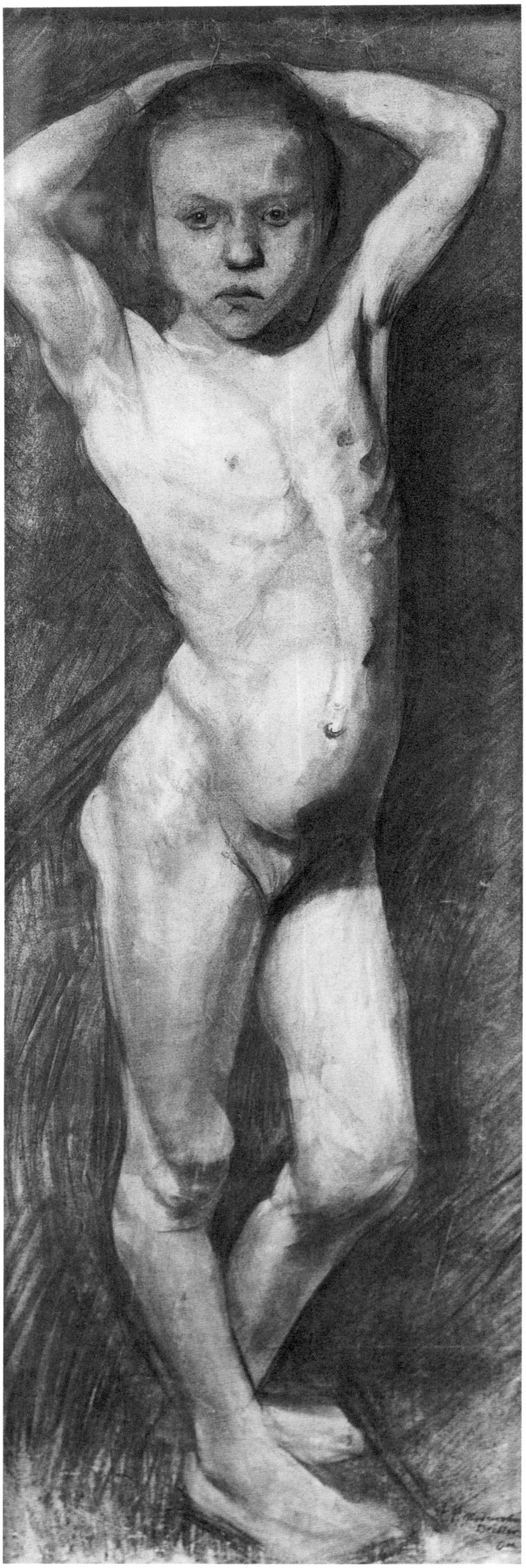

Standing Girl Nude, Hands Crossed behind Her Head, 1898

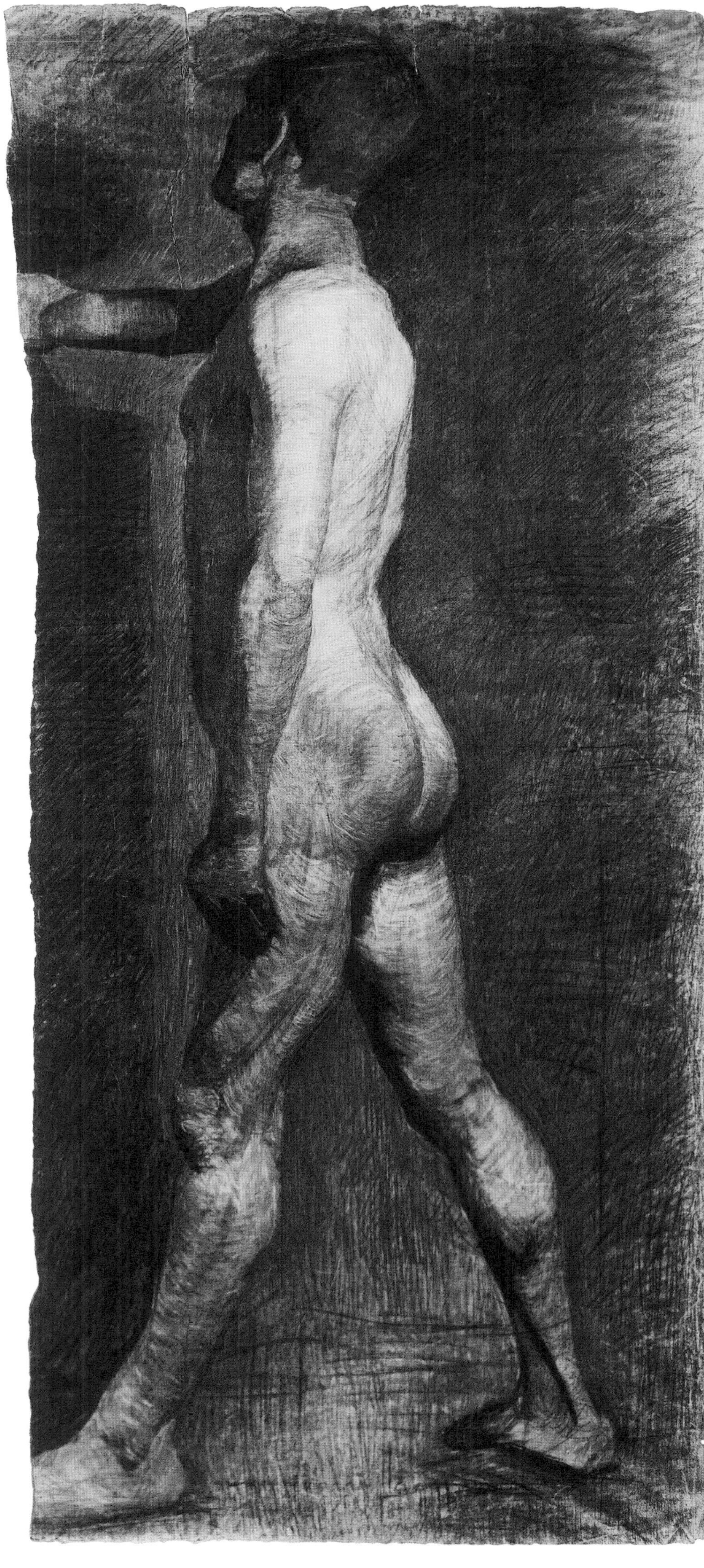

Standing Male Nude Facing Left, 1898

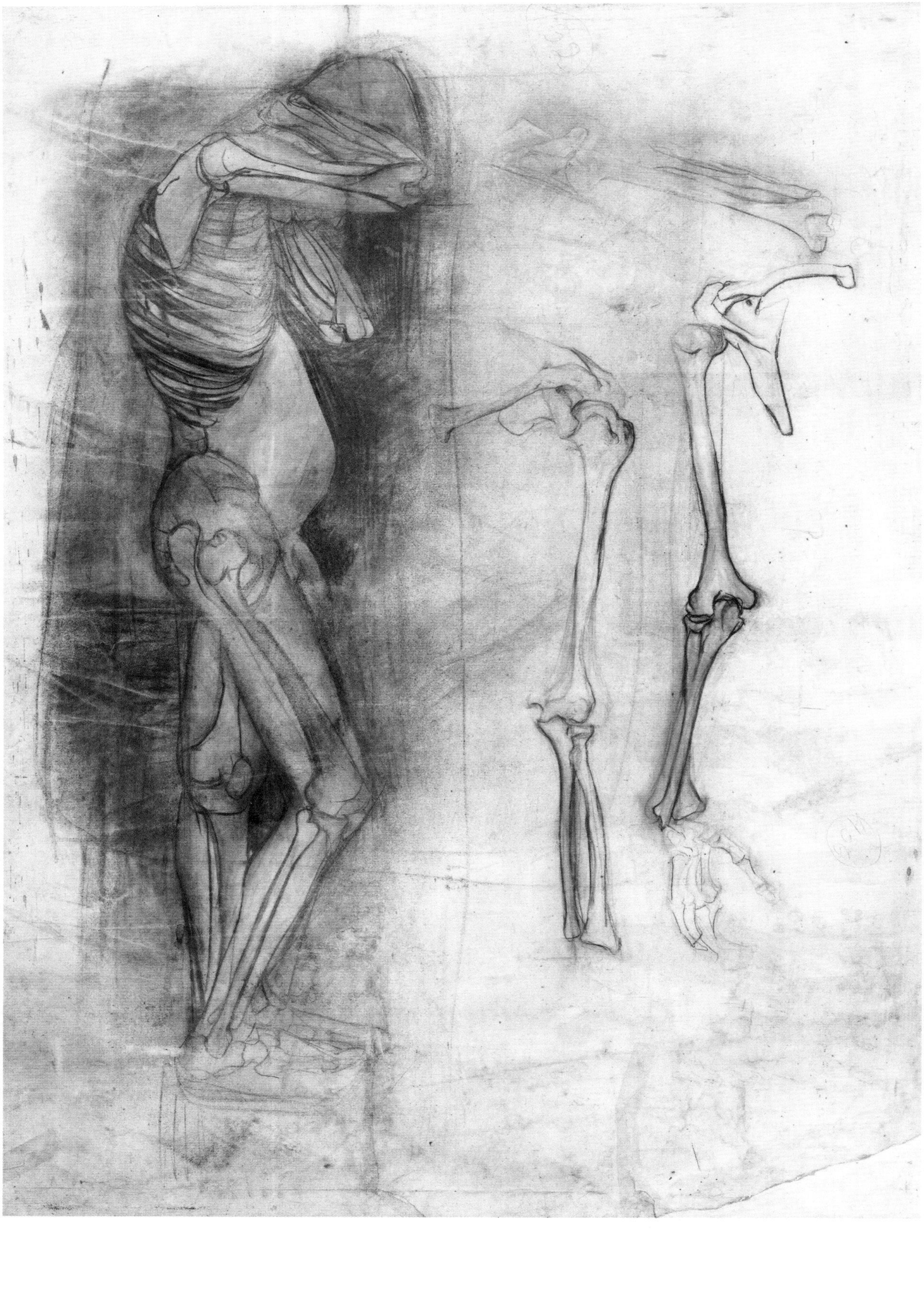

Standing Child Nude with the Skeleton Drawn in and Bone Studies, June 1899

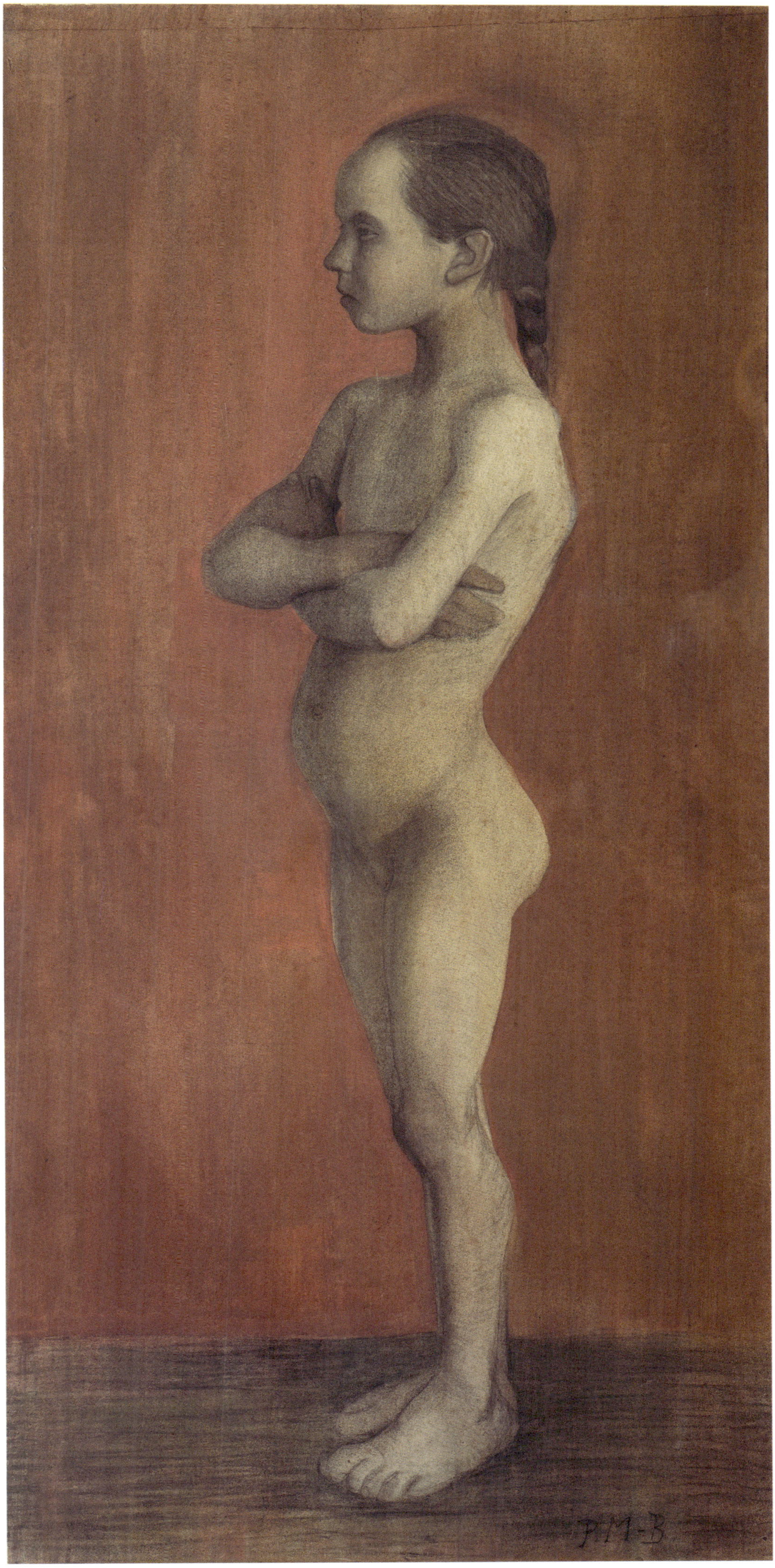

Standing Girl Nude Facing Left with Arms Crossed, 1898/99

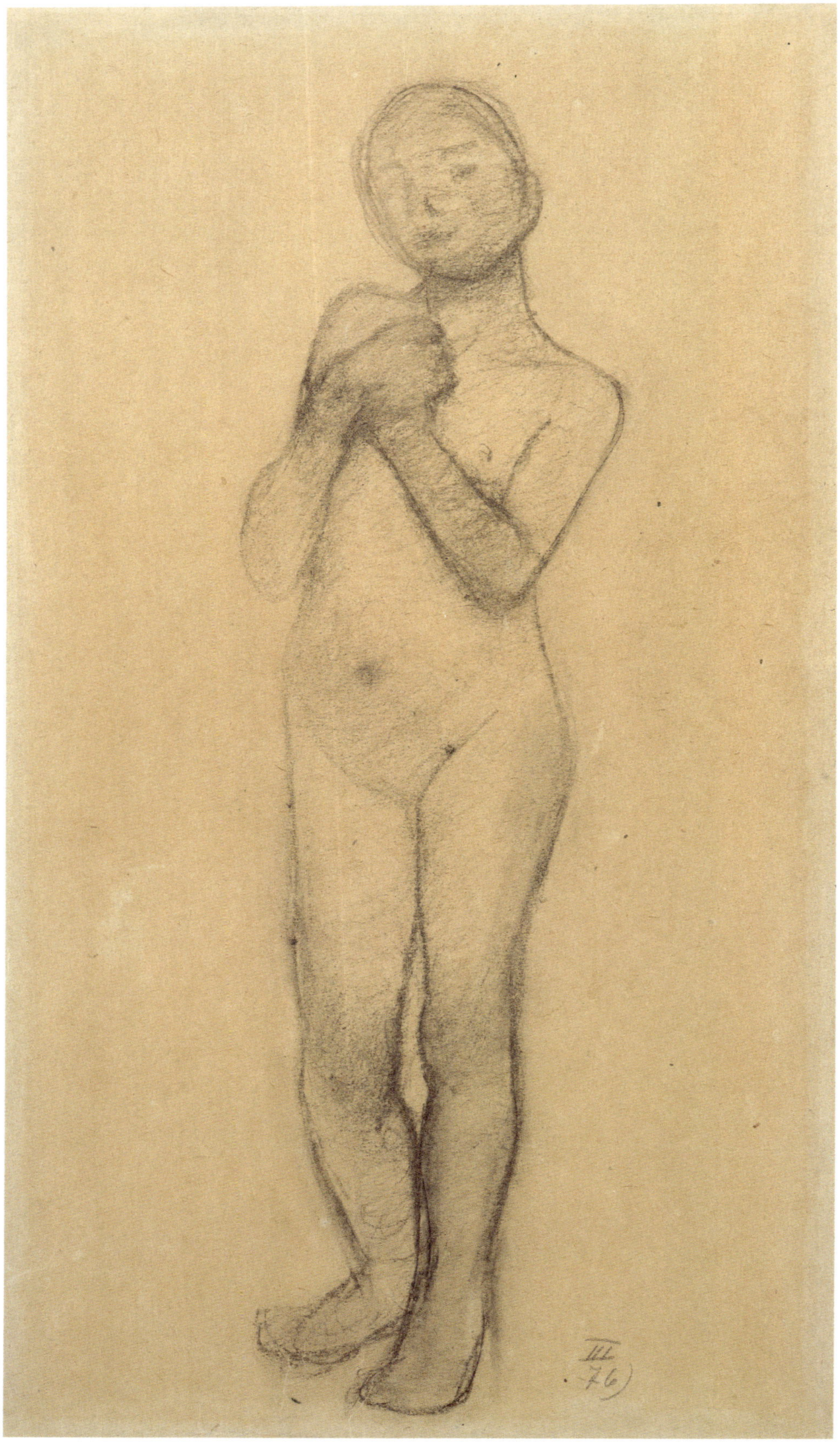

Standing Girl Nude with Hands Crossed, 1905/06

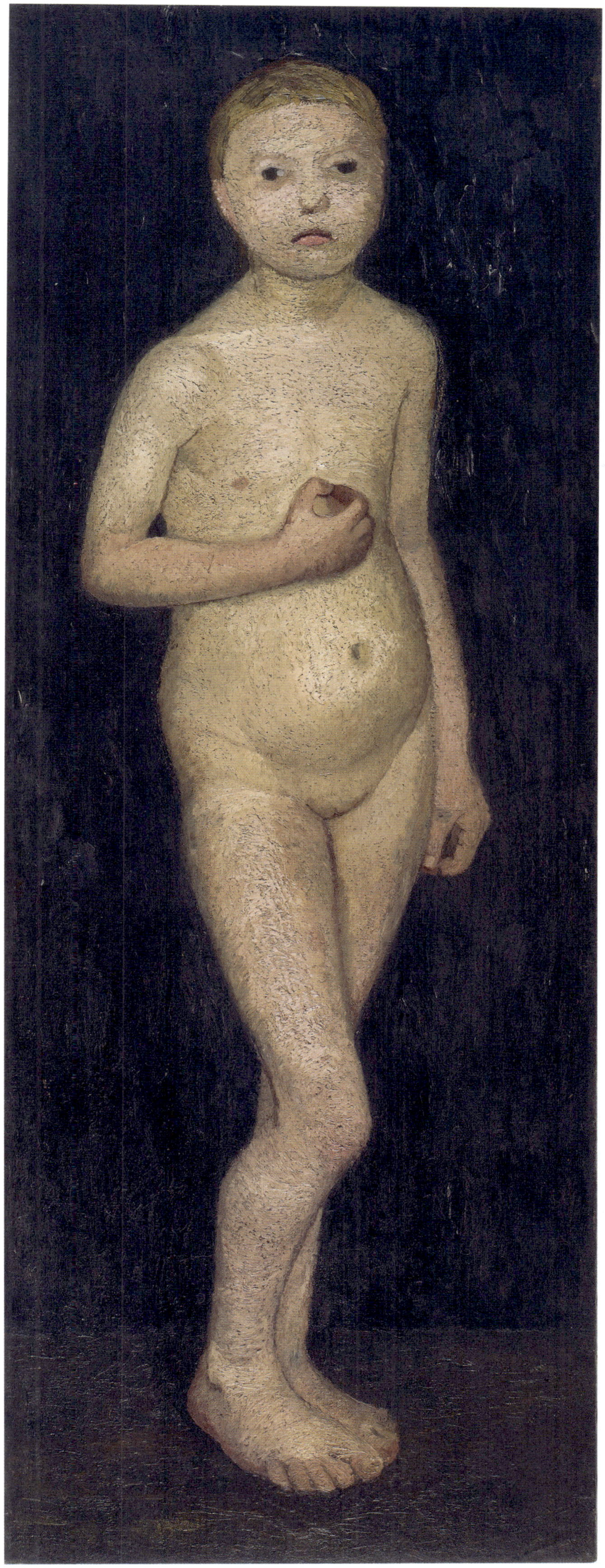

Large Standing Girl Nude, 1905/06

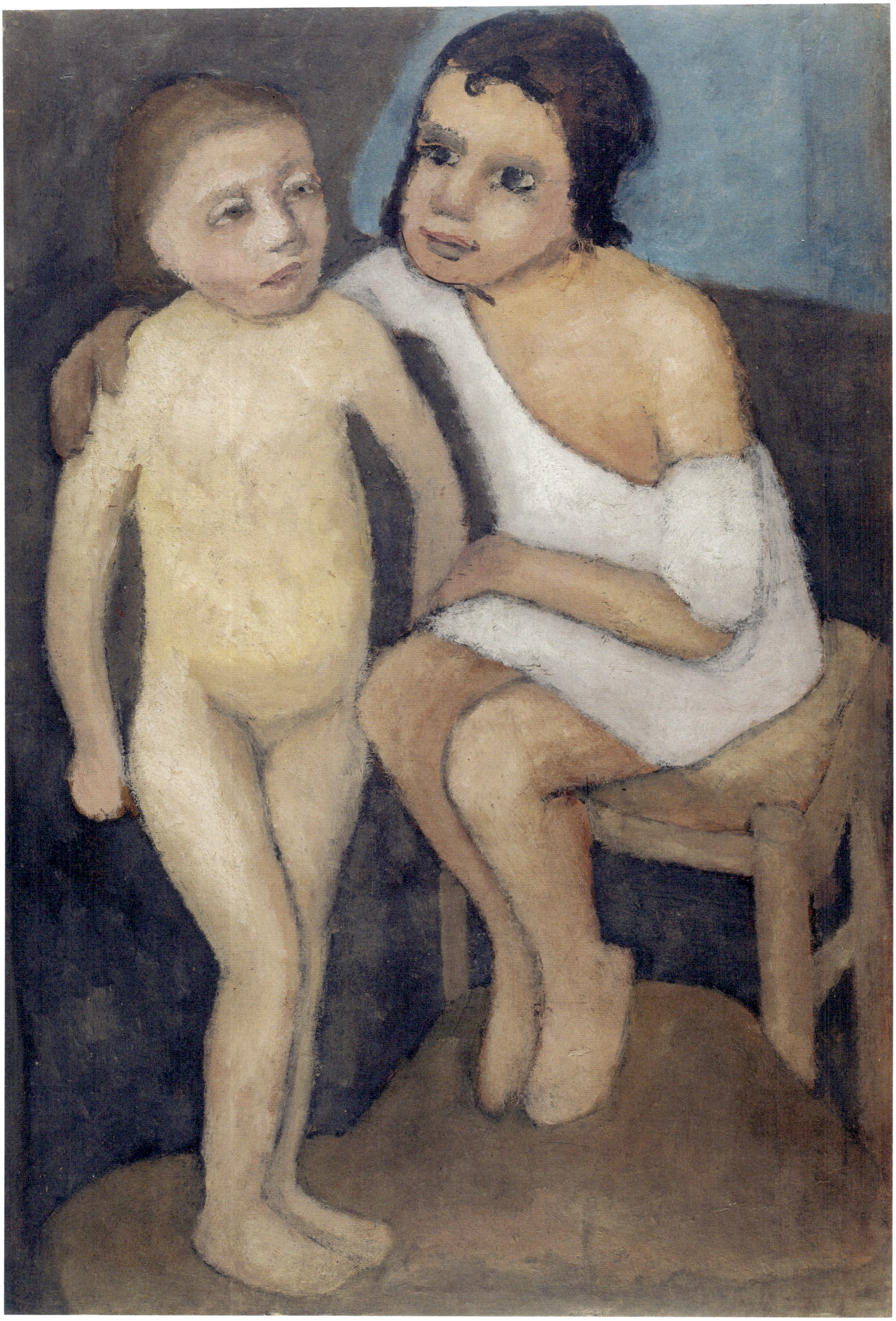

Seated Girl in White Shirt and Standing Girl Nude, May/June 1906

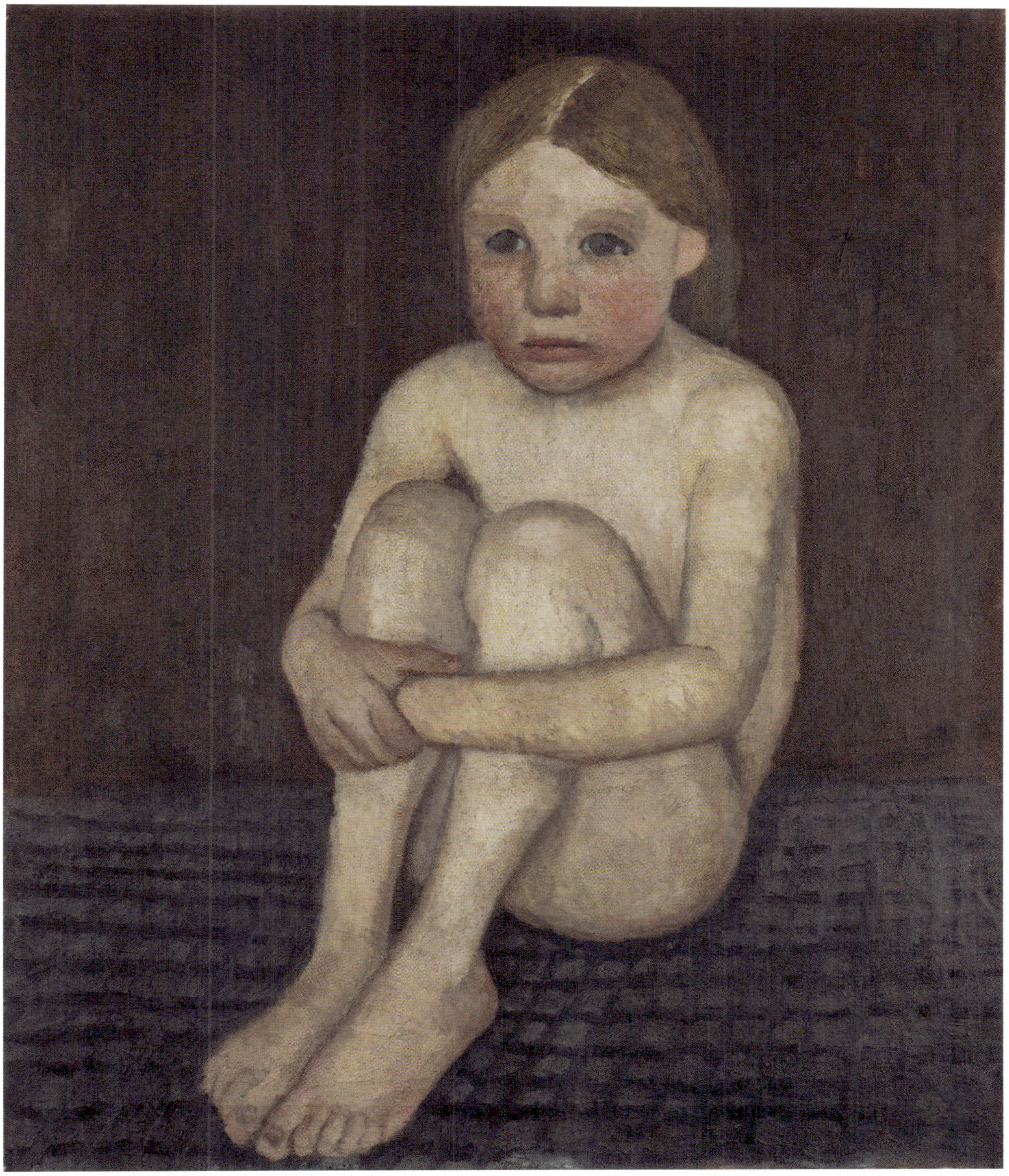

Seated Girl Nude with Her Legs Drawn Up I (Elsbeth), c. 1904

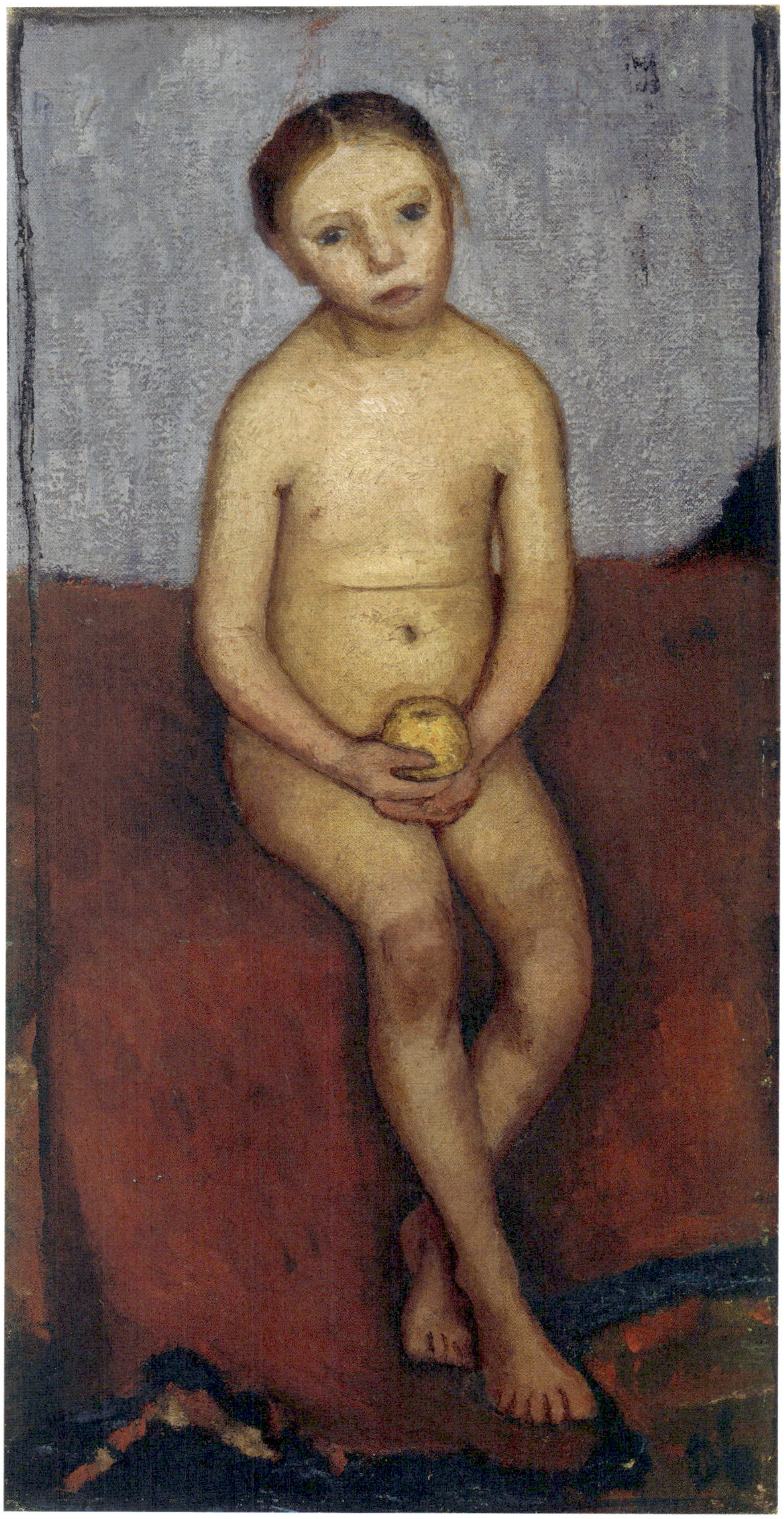

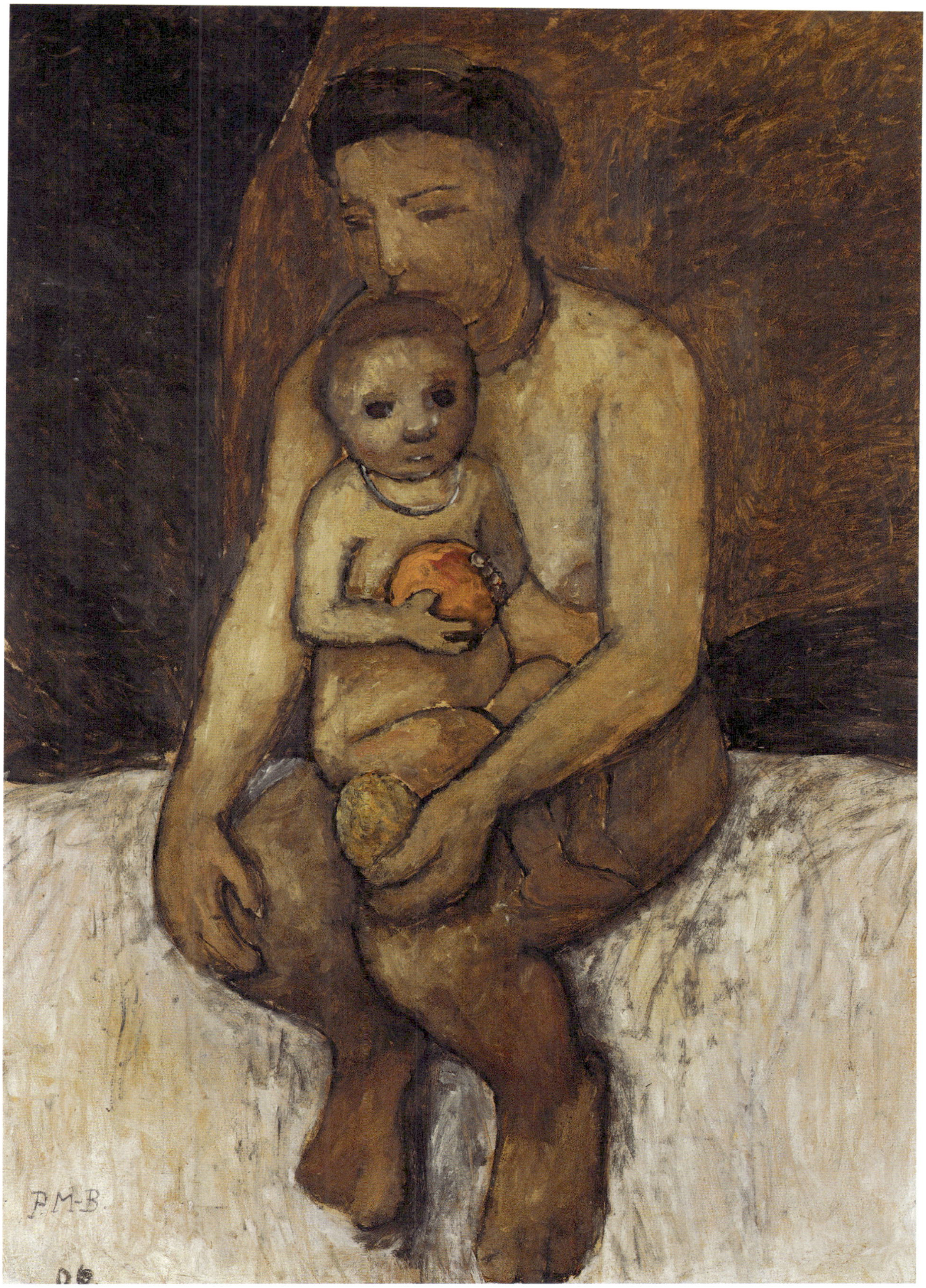

Seated Girl Nude with Apple, 1906

Seated Mother with Child in Her Lap, 1906

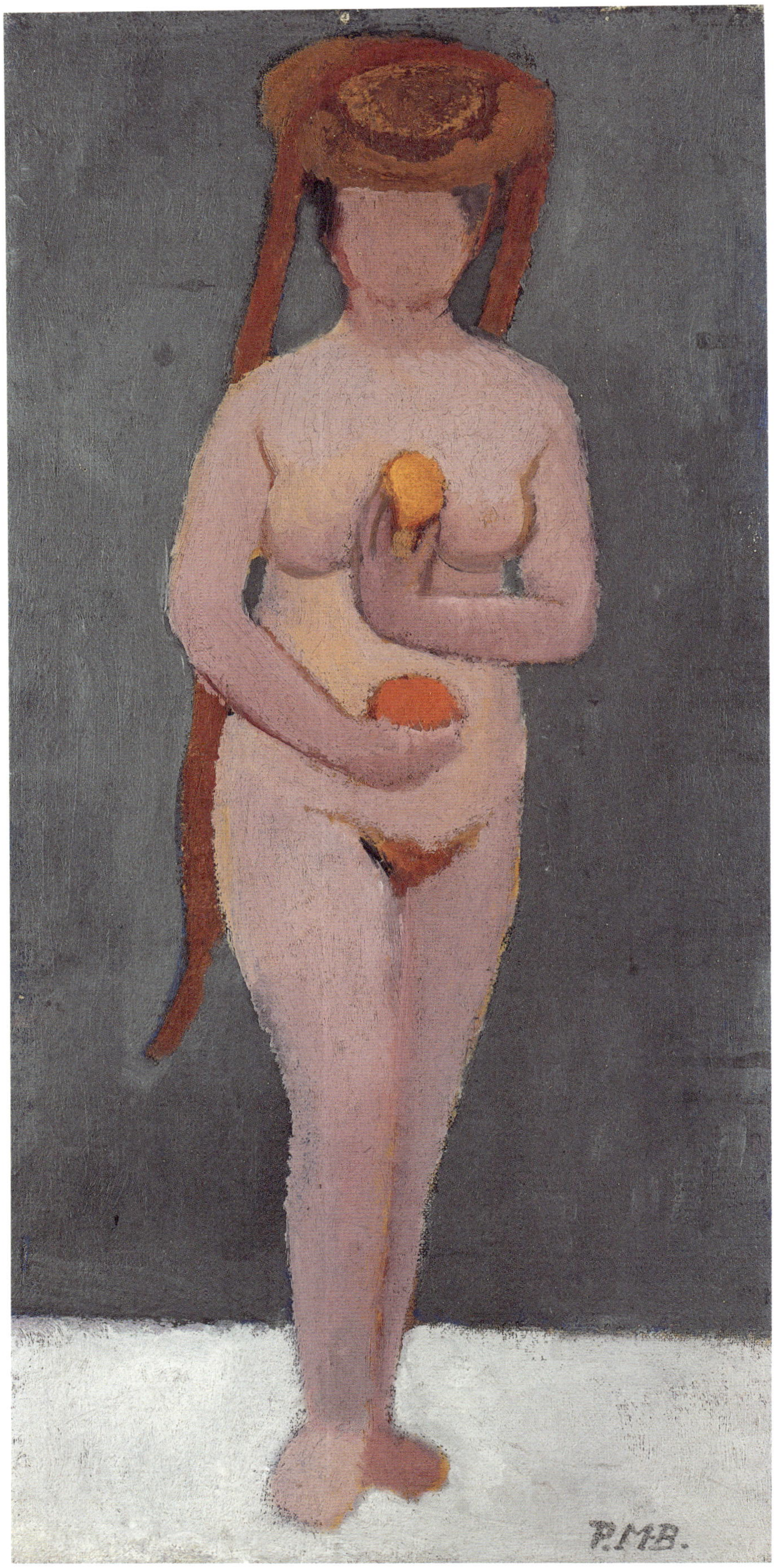

Self-Portrait as Standing Nude with Hat, 1906

Self-Portrait on the 6th Wedding Anniversary, 1906

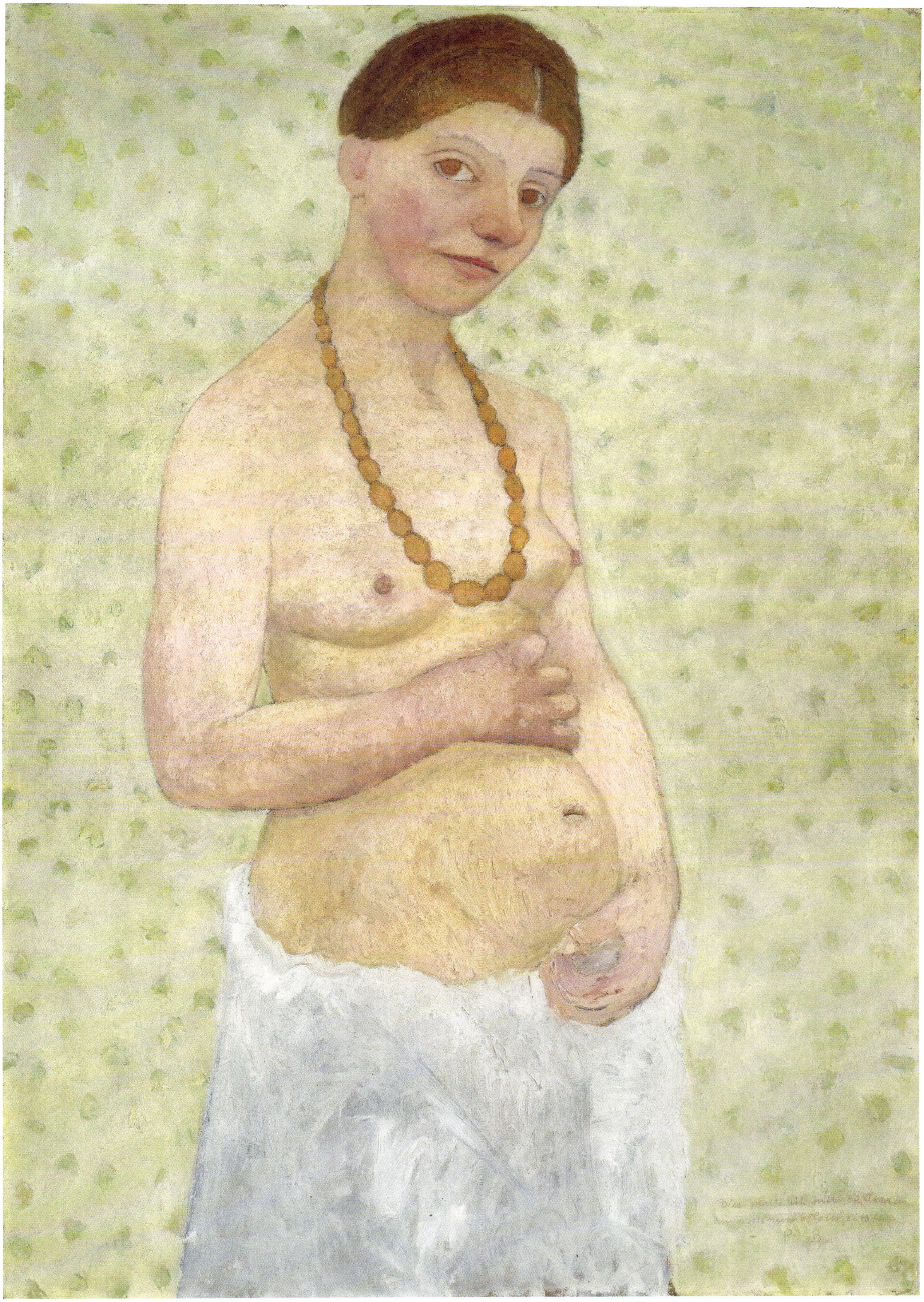

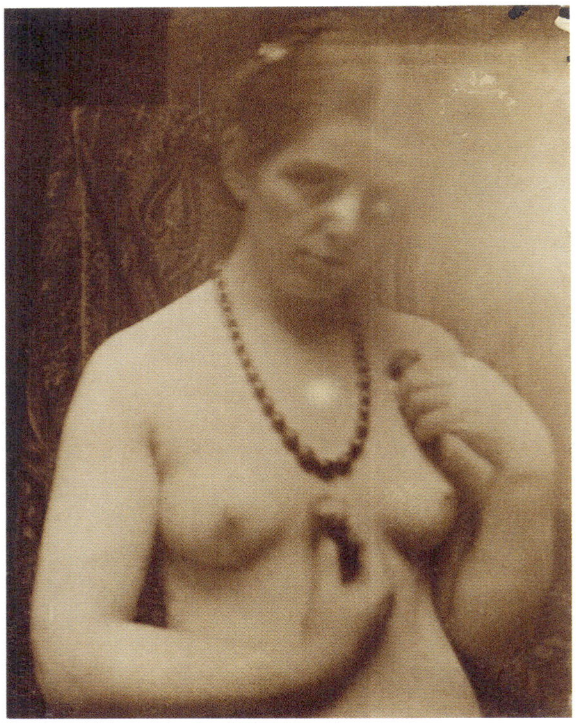

Paula Modersohn-Becker in a semi-nude pose, May/June 1906, photograph

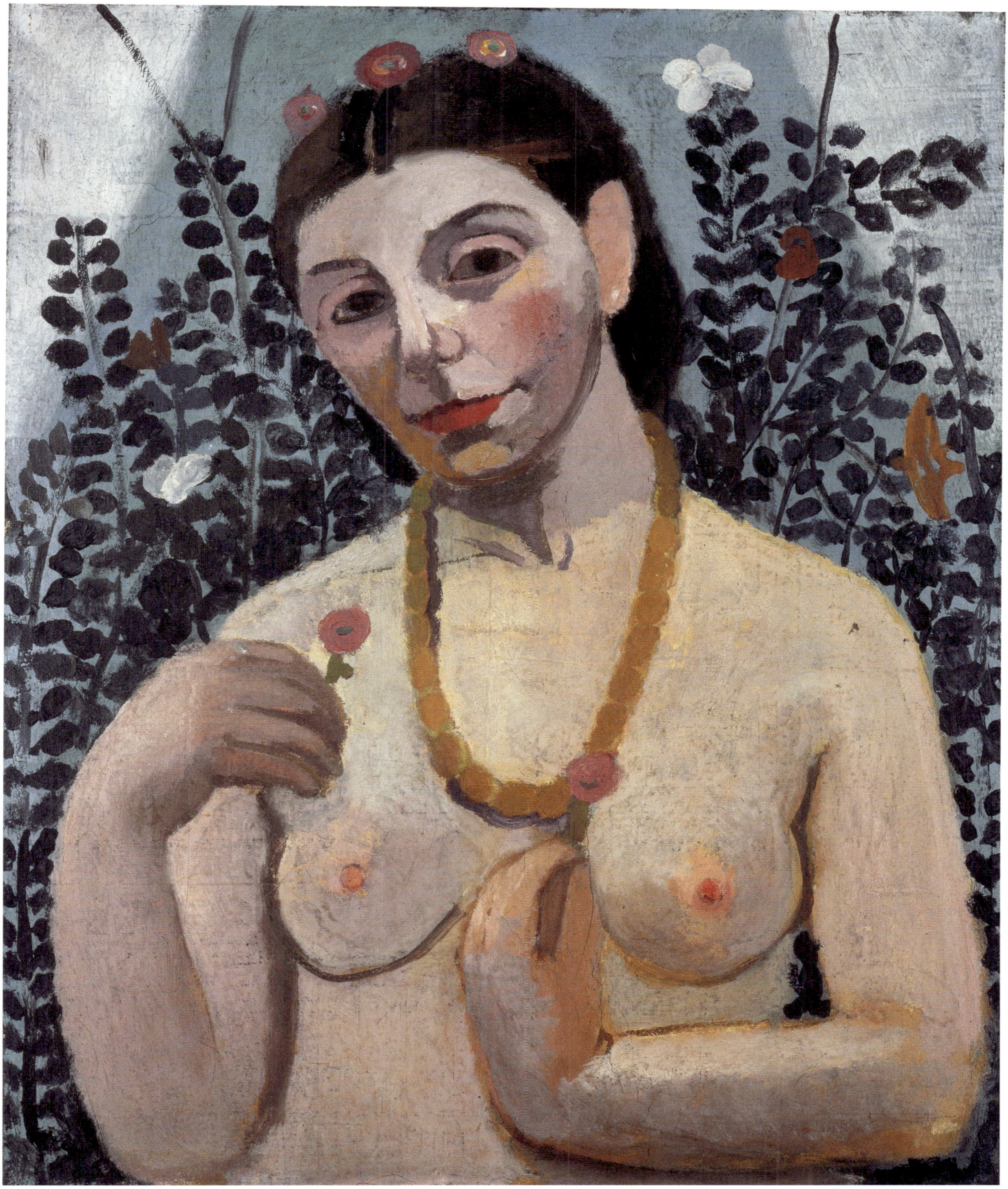

Semi-Nude Self-Portrait with Amber Necklace II, 1906

PAULA MODERSOHN-BECKER

REBECCA DUCKWITZ, SIMONE EWALD AND WOLFGANG WERNER

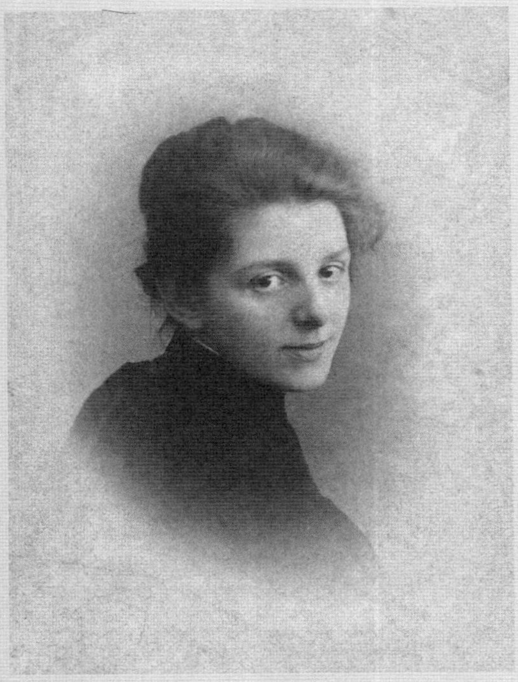

A LIFE BETWEEN LONDON, BERLIN, WORPSWEDE AND PARIS

1876–91 Minna Hermine Paula Becker is born in Dresden on 8 February 1876, the third of seven children. She is the daughter of the engineer Carl Woldemar Becker (1841–1901), construction manager of the Prussian Railway Administration in Bremen. Her mother, Mathilde (1852–1926), is from the aristocratic von Bültzingslöwen family in Thuringia. In 1888, the Becker family moves to Bremen and takes a keen interest in the city's literary and artistic life.

1892 Paula Becker spends seven months in England, staying with her aunt Marie Hill on a country estate near London and takes her first lessons in drawing from plaster models at the St John's Wood Art School in London.

1893–95 To follow her father's demand to render his daughter economically independent, she attends a teachers' training college in Bremen and graduates on 8 September 1895. Parallel to this, Paula Becker takes painting and drawing lessons from Bernhard Wiegandt. In April 1895, she reacts with enthusiasm to the first exhibition of works by the Worpswede painters in the Kunsthalle Bremen. She mentions Fritz Mackensen, Otto Modersohn and Heinrich Vogeler.

1896 In the spring, Paula Becker attends a four-week course at the Verein der Künstlerinnen und Kunstfreundinnen zu Berlin (Association of Berlin Women Artists and Art Lovers), founded in 1867. She returns to Berlin in October to embark on an eighteen-month training

Paula Becker, c. 1895

programme. Her free time is mostly spent visiting museums: "I now feel completely at home with the Germans and Holbein, but Rembrandt remains the greatest." Summer trip to Hindelang in the Allgäu region with a stop in Munich to visit the Pinakothek and the Schack Gallery.

1897 In February 1897, she joins the portrait painting class of the Swedish-German painter Jeanna Bauck (1840–1926), who has a lasting influence on her. Paula Becker frequently visits exhibitions of contemporary art at the galleries of Schulte, Gurlitt and Keller & Reiner, but also studies the classical canon and has drawings by Michelangelo and Botticelli's illustrations for Dante's *Divine Comedy* presented to her at the Kupferstich-kabinett in Berlin. From July to August, she stays in the Worpswede artist's colony for the first time. At the beginning of October, she travels to Dresden for the "Internationale Kunst-Ausstellung" of works by, among others, Degas, Monet, Pissarro, Sisley, Böcklin, Hodler, Klinger, Segantini and the Worpswede artists. At the beginning of December, she travels to Vienna and visits museums and the Liechtenstein Gallery. In her letters, she mentions Titian, Rubens, Dürer, Cranach, Holbein, Leonardo and Van Dyck.

1898 Paula Becker continues her studies in Berlin. In March/April, she is delighted by the exhibition of artists' lithographs at the Kunstgewerbemuseum, featuring works by Klinger, Menzel, Thoma, Manet, Pissarro, Sérusier, Signac, Toulouse-Lautrec, Vallotton, Munch and others. At the Galerie Gurlitt, she sees paintings by the Hungarian Nabis artist Rippl-Rónai and at Galerie Schulte the Berlin association of eleven artists known as the "Vereinigung der XI", including Liebermann and Klinger; she mentions Leistikow. Munch's work is exhibited at Keller & Reiner in April. She visits Klinger's studio on a trip to Leipzig. At the end of May, she finishes her studies in Berlin and spends the summer in Norway with her uncle Wulf von Bültzingslöwen. She settles in the Worpswede artist's colony in September. On her first evening in Worpswede, she writes to her aunt Cora von Bültzingslöwen: "I enjoy my life with every breath I take, and in the distance, Paris glows and shines." Fritz Mackensen, who has also accepted Clara Westhoff and Marie Bock as students, corrects Paula Becker's life-size figures in charcoal and coloured chalk. She befriends the sculptor Clara Westhoff.

1899 Paula Becker fills her sketchbooks with landscape drawings, figure studies and compositional sketches. She also works on landscape paintings and a series of etchings, which she prints by hand on a printing press at Heinrich Vogeler's home, known as Barkenhoff. She takes a keen interest in literature and mainly reads, alongside older works, Jens Peter Jacobsen and Henrik Ibsen. In August, she travels to Switzerland. The return journey takes her through Munich, Nuremberg and Leipzig, where Clara Westhoff works with Klinger, as well as to Dresden for the German Art Exhibition, in which the Worpswede artists are participating. In December, the first exhibition of several of her studies is shown at the Kunsthalle Bremen, together with works by Marie Bock and Clara Westhoff. It receives a scathing review by the painter and art critic Arthur Fitger.

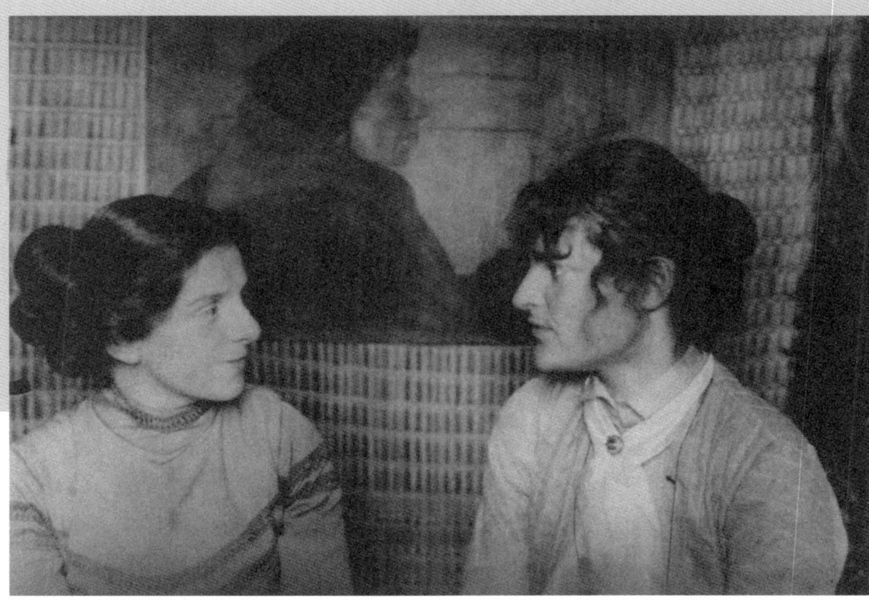

Paula Becker and Clara Westhoff in Paula Becker's studio, c. 1899

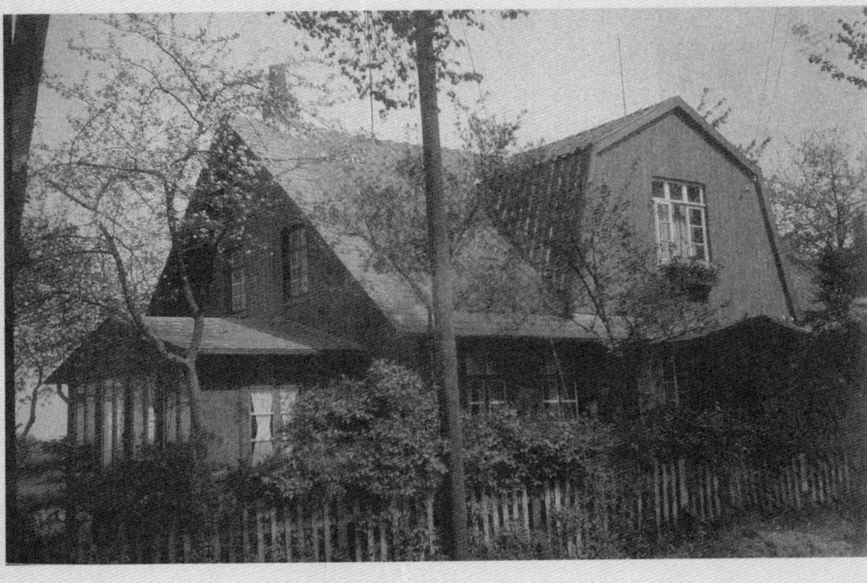

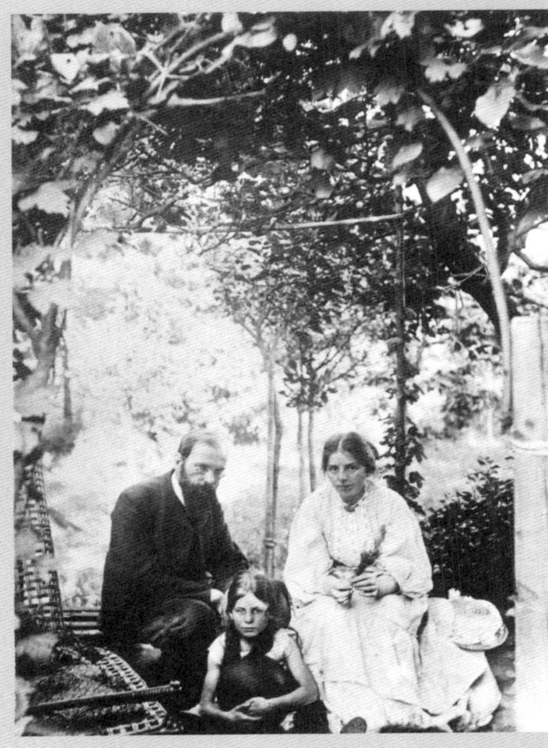

1900 On New Year's Eve, Paula Becker travels to Paris for the first time. There, she meets Clara Westhoff, who wishes to study at the sculpture school established by Auguste Rodin. She moves into a studio at 9 Rue Campagne Première and studies in the nude class at the Académie Colarossi, where she wins the medal in the semester competition. Together with Clara Westhoff, she also attends anatomy lessons at the École des Beaux-Arts. At art dealer Ambroise Vollard's gallery, she discovers paintings by Paul Cézanne, which make a strong impression on her. In her letters, she mentions Titian, Botticelli, Fra Angelico, Velázquez, Rembrandt, Holbein and Donatello, whose work she studies during her frequent visits to the Louvre. She also writes about the more recent artists Corot, Rousseau, Millet, Daubigny, Degas, Puvis de Chavannes, Courbet and Monet.

In Georges Petit's gallery, Paula Becker sees works by the Breton painters Lucien Simon and Charles Cottet. The *Revue Blanche* holds an extensive Seurat exhibition in March. She encounters Emil Nolde and the Dachau painter Emmi Walther. In June, the Worpswede artists Otto Modersohn, Fritz and Hermine Overbeck and Marie Bock travel to Paris to visit the World's Fair and see Rodin's sculpture pavilion at the Pont de l'Alma. Otto Modersohn's wife, Helene, dies in Worpswede. Paula Becker and Clara Westhoff return to Worpswede at the end of June. At Vogeler's Barkenhoff, the circle of artist friends who call themselves the "Family" – Otto Modersohn, Paula Becker, Heinrich Vogeler, his future wife, Martha Schröder, Clara Westhoff, Marie Bock and Paula Becker's sisters, Milly and Herma – meet in the "White Hall". The poets Rainer Maria Rilke and Carl Hauptmann are frequent guests. In September, Paula Becker and Otto Modersohn become engaged. Apart from a few figure paintings, she almost exclusively paints landscapes.

1901 In January and February, at her parents' request, she takes cooking lessons in Berlin. While visiting museums, she studies and copies works by Rembrandt, Velázquez, Verrocchio, Dürer, Hans Baldung, the Master of Messkirch and Goya. In the Berlin

The home of Paula and Otto Modersohn in Worpswede, around 1902

Paula, Otto and Elsbeth Modersohn at Barkenhof, around 1904, photo: Ernst Portig

galleries, she sees the Daumier exhibition at Cassirer's and paintings by Arnold Böcklin at the Galerie Gurlitt.

On May 25, Paula Becker marries Otto Modersohn, who brings his three-year-old daughter, Elsbeth, into the marriage. Their honeymoon takes them to Berlin, Dresden and Schreiberhau, where they visit Carl Hauptmann, then to Prague, Munich and Dachau. She keeps her former room in the house of the farmer Brünjes and converts it into a studio.

1902 In her paintings, she focuses mainly on figures in the landscape and occasionally paints with Otto Modersohn in front of the same motif. She engages intensively with her own painting and reflects on colour and composition: "[…] I dream of movement in colour, of gentle shimmering, vibration, of one object setting another in motion through colour."

1903 In February, she travels to Paris for a second time. Again, she enrolls at the Académie Colarossi for nude drawing classes. Together with Rainer Maria Rilke and Clara Rilke-Westhoff, she visits various exhibitions and the art dealers on Rue Laffitte. At the Hôtel Drouot, they view Japanese paintings and sculptures from the Hayashi Collection. She frequently draws at the Louvre. In addition to Rembrandt and Veronese, she is interested in antiquity, especially the late antique Fayum portraits. After a visit to the Musée du Luxembourg, she mentions Manet, Renoir, Zuloaga, Cottet and Degas. On Rilke's recommendation, she visits Rodin, who shows her his watercolours. In March, she returns to Worpswede. The Modersohn family spends the summer on the isle of Amrum. In the winter of 1903/04, she produces only a few paintings and reads a lot of French literature.

1904 The distance between Paula Modersohn-Becker and her Worpswede colleagues increases. In a critical examination of her previous work, she seeks new pictorial forms in her drawings. A central theme in her paintings from 1904/05 is figures integrated into landscapes, such as *Girl Playing the Flute in a Birch Forest*, 1905 (fig. p. 41).

In the summer, Paula Modersohn-Becker and Otto Modersohn travel to Dresden via Berlin (*Große Kunstausstellung*, with a major retrospective of 19th-century French masters), then to Kassel and Braunschweig (Rembrandt).

1905 During her third trip to Paris in February, she registers for a month at the Académie Julian, where Gauguin and the Nabis had studied in the 1890s, to "paint nudes from eight to eleven". Through Rilke, she meets the Norwegian writer couple Johann and Ellen Bojer. She visits the studios of the Nabis artists Édouard Vuillard and Maurice Denis, as well as Charles Cottet; for the first time, she sees sculptures by Aristide Maillol. She asks Otto Modersohn to send her addresses of private collections in Paris from Meier-Graefe's

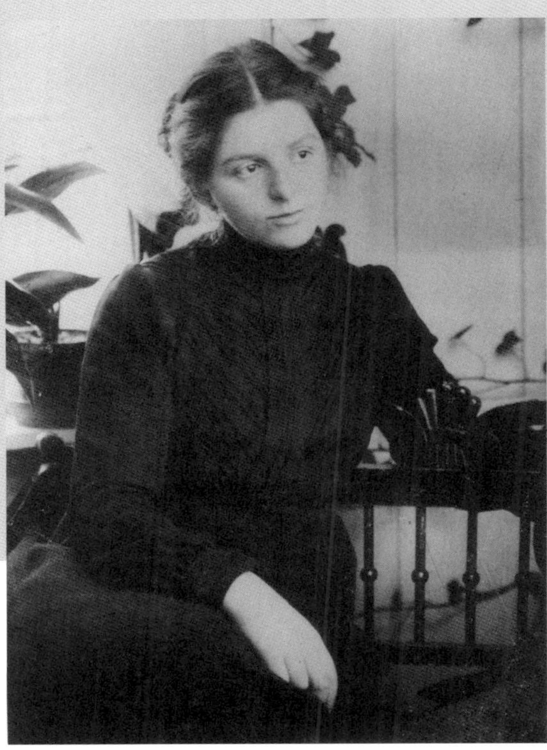

Paula Modersohn-Becker on the veranda of her house (detail), around 1901, photo: Atelier Schaub, Hamburg

Entwicklungsgeschichte der modernen Kunst (History of the Development of Modern Art, 1904). At the Salon des Indépendants, she sees paintings by Matisse and the Fauves, as well as the retrospective shows of Seurat and Van Gogh. At the end of March, Otto Modersohn, Milly Becker and Martha and Heinrich Vogeler come to Paris. Together, they visit Gustave Fayet's Gauguin collection and take a trip to Meudon to see Rodin. After her return to Worpswede in April, she asks her sister Herma in Paris to send her the prices of various publications about Gauguin, including *Noa-Noa*. In November, Heinrich Vogeler, Paula Modersohn-Becker and Otto Modersohn visit Karl Ernst Osthaus and his wife at their Museum Folkwang in Hagen. Rainer Maria Rilke stays in Worpswede for Christmas and acquires the painting *Infant with Mother's Hand* during a visit to her studio. At the turn of the year, Paula Modersohn-Becker and Otto Modersohn travel to Schreiberhau at Carl Hauptmann's invitation. There they meet, among others, the sociologist Werner Sombart and the painter Otto Mueller on a trip to Dresden.

1906 The return journey from Schreiberhau takes them through Dresden and Berlin. In Berlin, they see the *Centennial Exhibition of German Art from 1775–1875* at the Königliche Nationalgalerie. She mentions Leibl, Trübner, Böcklin, Feuerbach and Marées. On 23 February, Paula Modersohn-Becker moves to Paris and leaves Otto Modersohn. She now wants to fully devote herself to her work, free from external constraints, and implement what she has gradually developed in her studies and drawings over the last few years. On her decision to leave Worpswede, she comments to Carl Hauptmann: "Those were probably the five most beautiful years of my life, the ones I spent in Worpswede," but she concludes with the postscript: "It is too limited there for me." (22 April 1906)

She moves into an artist's studio at 14 Avenue du Maine in early March and, for a month, attends the anatomy courses and a life drawing class at the École des Beaux-Arts, where women are now permitted. The Druet Gallery is exhibiting Matisse paintings, and Vollard is once again showing works by Cézanne. She writes to Otto Modersohn about her visits to the exhibitions: "I have seen magnificent Courbets; I am sorry that he is currently in vogue. However, I find him more impressive than Manet and Monet."

At the beginning of April, she goes on excursions with Rainer Maria Rilke, occasionally accompanied by Ellen Key and the Bojer couple. She paints portraits of Rainer Maria Rilke and Werner Sombart, who is also staying in Paris. In mid-April, she spends Easter with her sister Herma in St Malo in Brittany, where she sees the brightly coloured sculptures that the Abbé Fouré began carving into the rocks near Rothéneuf in the late 19th century. The sculptures are one of the sources of inspiration for her later figure paintings. Back in Paris, Paula Modersohn-Becker and Rilke, among other artists like Maillol, visit the unveiling of Rodin's *The Thinker* in front of the Panthéon on 21 April. She meets the sculptor Bernhard Hoetger and his wife, Helene (Lee). On 4 May, Hoetger visits Paula Modersohn-Becker in her studio and is immensely impressed by her talent. This is followed by weeks of intense work on the monumental figure compositions, including

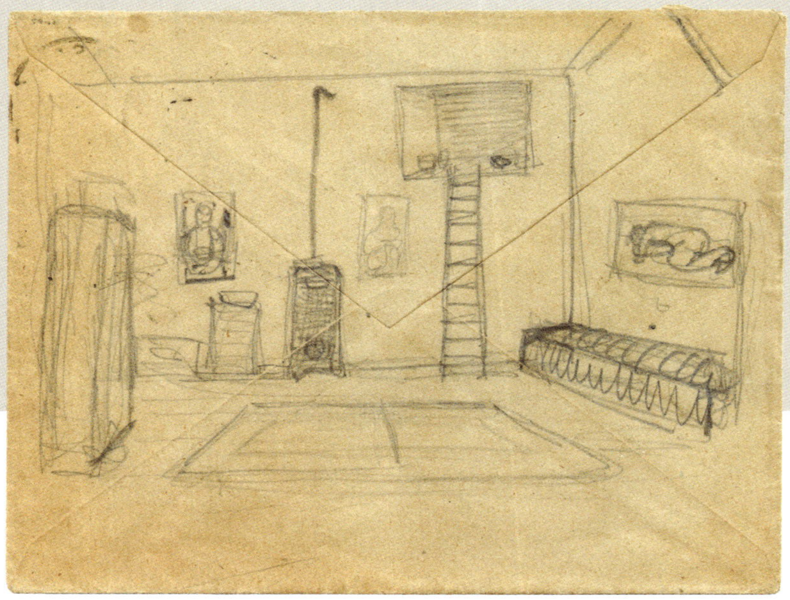

Sketch by Paula Modersohn-Becker of her last Paris studio, at 49 Boulevard Montparnasse, 1906, with the paintings *Portrait of Lee Hoetger in front of a Floral Background*, *Woman with Cat and Parrot* and *Reclining Mother with Child II* on the walls

the *Self-Portrait* (fig. p. 83) completed on 25 May 1906 with the programmatic inscription: "I painted this at the age of thirty on my sixth wedding anniversary," which she signed P. B. – Paula Becker. Her sister Herma, who is also staying in Paris, tells her mother: "Her thirtieth year will give her pause for thought, as she herself has set it as a goal for her painting [...]." She begins to prepare her nude compositions in a large number of rapidly sketched, very abbreviated drawings. Her models are Italian mothers with their children, whom she finds on the model market in the Rue de la Grande-Chaumière at the beginning of each week. In June–July, she makes large paintings of standing or reclining mothers with children (fig. pp. 70/71). She tells her friend Martha Vogeler in Worpswede: "I love sleeping between my works and waking up between them in the morning. I paint life-size nudes and still lifes with trust in God and self-confidence."

Inspired by the pictorial world of the painter Henri Rousseau, whose studio she had visited with the Hoetger couple, she begins work in August on the large half-figure *painting Lee Hoetger in front of a Floral Background* (fig. p. 51), which, according to a letter by her sister Milly, she probably intends to exhibit at the Salon des Indépendants in the spring of 1907. On 12 August, she tells Heinrich Vogeler about another portrait of Lee Hoetger (fig. p. 56): "I am currently painting Frau Hoetger's portrait. She can look absolutely magnificent and grave; with an enormous crown of hair, blonde, splendidly shaped." These tectonically constructed works mark the beginning of her new protocubist phase with the *Kneeling Mother with Child at Her Breast* and the half-length *Semi-Nude of an Italian Woman with a Plate in Her Raised Hand*. In the autumn, she works on the mask-like *Self-Portrait with Lemon* and the *Self-Portrait Half-Turned to the Right, Her Hand on Her Chin*. The inspiration for these is probably the African masks that she had seen during a visit to the Musée de l'Homme with Bernhard Hoetger. She and Hoetger also visit Paul Gauguin's retrospective at the Salon d'Automne. At the end of October, Otto Modersohn comes to Paris to spend the winter with his wife. During this time, she rents a new studio at 49 Boulevard Montparnasse. In November, the Kunsthalle Bremen shows four of her paintings in the exhibition of Worpswede artists, which subsequently travels to the Galerie Gurlitt in Berlin.

1907 Before returning to Worpswede at the end of March, she sees Auguste Pellerin's collection of works by Cézanne. In Worpswede that summer, in addition to still lifes, she creates the monumental figure paintings of the *Old Poorhouse Woman in the Garden with Glass Ball and Poppies* (fig. p. 59) and the *Old Peasant Woman with Hands Crossed on Her Chest*. She shares her new thoughts on the colour composition with Bernhard Hoetger: "I have not done much work this summer [...]. In its concept, all the work has probably remained much the same. However, the execution, I think, is quite another matter. What I want to produce is something compelling, something full – an excitement and intoxication of colours – something powerful. The paintings I made in Paris are too cool and too solitary and empty [...]."

As requested, Rilke sends her the catalogue of the Salon d'Automne, where a Cézanne retrospective had taken place. Clara Rilke-Westhoff writes to Modersohn-Becker on 18 October that she intends to visit her soon and read to her from the letters Rilke had sent her with descriptions of the Cézanne exhibition. Modersohn-Becker replies: "My mind has been so much occupied these days by the thought of Cézanne, of how he is one of the three or four powerful artists who have affected me like a thunderstorm. Do you remember 1900 at Vollard? [...] Come soon and bring the letters. Come right away, Monday if you can possibly make it, for I hope to be otherwise occupied soon. If it were not absolutely necessary for me to be here now, I should be in Paris." Their daughter, Mathilde, is born on 2 November. On 20 November, Paula Modersohn-Becker dies of pulmonary embolism.

LIST OF WORKS

Catalogues raisonnés

Busch/Werner
Paula Modersohn Becker. Werkverzeichnis der Gemälde, 2 vols., ed. by Günter Busch, Wolfgang Werner and Milena Schicketanz, Munich 1998

Röver-Kann/Werner
Paula Modersohn-Becker. Werkverzeichnis der Handzeichnungen, 2 vols., ed. by Anne Röver-Kann and Wolfgang Werner, Munich 2023

The works are listed in chronological order according to their catalogue raisoneé numbers.

PAULA MODERSOHN-BECKER
(1876–1907)

Goblet and Cylinder, 1891
Charcoal
31.6 × 42.7 cm
Paula-Modersohn-Becker-Stiftung, Bremen
Röver-Kann/Werner E I/1
Fig. p. 13

Drawing Based on a Bust of a Greek Youth with His Mouth Open, 1892
Charcoal
58 × 41 cm
Paula-Modersohn-Becker-Stiftung, Bremen
Röver-Kann/Werner E I/11
Fig. p. 12

Self-Portrait by Lamplight, 1896
Red chalk, heightened in white, on yellowish paper
32.7 × 24.3 cm
Paula-Modersohn-Becker-Stiftung, Bremen
Röver-Kann/Werner A 22 verso
Fig. p. 11

Self-Portrait, c. 1897
Pastel on brown-grey cardboard
45.8 × 30.8 cm
Paula-Modersohn-Becker-Stiftung, Bremen
Röver-Kann/Werner E II/101
Fig. p. 17

Portrait of a Lady Wearing a Hat and Veil, 1897
Pastel on grey cardboard
48.6 × 62.3 cm
Kunsthalle Bremen – Der Kunstverein in Bremen
Röver-Kann/Werner E II/110
Fig. p. 15

Bust Portrait of a Man Facing Half-Right, c. 1897
Charcoal and coloured chalk on grey cardboard
57 × 43.5 cm
Paula-Modersohn-Becker-Stiftung, Bremen, on loan from a private collection
Röver-Kann/Werner E II/111
Fig. p. 16

Lady with Hat in a Deckchair, 1896/97
Gouache on grey paper
31.8 × 47.8 cm
Paula-Modersohn-Becker-Stiftung, Bremen
Röver-Kann/Werner E II/150
Fig. p. 14

Row of Trees, 1897
Gouache
30.8 × 49.3 cm
Paula-Modersohn-Becker-Stiftung, Bremen
Röver-Kann/Werner E II/155
Fig. pp. 36/37

Night-Time Landscape, 1897
Oil on paper
29.8 × 60 cm
Paula-Modersohn-Becker-Stiftung, Bremen
Röver-Kann/Werner E II/179
Fig. p. 36

Self-Portrait, 1897/98
Oil tempera on cardboard
28.2 × 23 cm
Kunsthalle Bremen – Der Kunstverein in Bremen
Busch/Werner 2
Fig. p. 20

Bust Portrait of an Old Woman with White Cloth, 1897
Oil tempera on cardboard
69 × 48 cm
Paula-Modersohn-Becker-Stiftung, Bremen, on loan from a private collection
Busch/Werner 4
Fig. p. 27

Child's Head with White Cloth, c. 1897
Oil tempera on cardboard
31 × 37.2 cm
Private collection
Busch/Werner 6
Fig. p. 26

Girl with Fire Lilies, 1897
Oil tempera on canvas on cardboard
39.3 × 48 cm
Paula-Modersohn-Becker-Stiftung, Bremen
Busch/Werner 8
Fig. p. 45

Bust Portrait of a Girl in the Sun in front of a Wide Landscape, 1897
Oil tempera on cardboard
44.5 × 49 cm
Private collection
Busch/Werner 12
Fig. p. 30

Seated Old Woman, Her Hands in Her Lap, 1898/99
Charcoal, black chalk, red chalk and blue coloured pencil
82.5 × 49.8 cm
Paula-Modersohn-Becker-Stiftung, Bremen, on loan from a private collection
Röver-Kann/Werner E III/76
Fig. p. 23

Seated Old Blind Woman, 1898/99
Pastel over charcoal
73 × 46 cm
Arp Museum Bahnhof Rolandseck /
Stiftung Rau für UNICEF
Röver-Kann/Werner E III/84
Fig. p. 19

Standing Girl Nude Facing Left with Arms Crossed, 1898/99
Charcoal, red chalk and green pastel pencil
136 × 68 cm
Paula-Modersohn-Becker-Stiftung, Bremen, on loan from a private collection
Röver-Kann/Werner E III/86
Fig. p. 75

Standing Child Nude with the Skeleton Drawn in and Bone Studies, June 1899
Charcoal
145 × 111 cm
Paula-Modersohn-Becker-Stiftung, Bremen
Röver-Kann/Werner E III/89
Fig. p. 74

Standing Male Nude Facing Left, 1898
Charcoal
189.5 × 84.5 cm
Paula-Modersohn-Becker-Stiftung, Bremen
Röver-Kann/Werner E III/91
Fig. p. 73

Standing Girl Nude, Hands Crossed behind Her Head, 1898
Charcoal
124.5 × 41.5 cm
Paula Modersohn-Becker Museum, Bremen
Röver-Kann/Werner E III/94
Fig. p. 72

Woman with Hands Folded in Her Lap, 1898
Oil tempera on cardboard on wood
44.5 × 31 cm
Paula-Modersohn-Becker-Stiftung, Bremen, on loan from a private collection
Busch/Werner 19
Fig. p. 22

Bust Portrait of a Woman in Profile to the Right, c. 1898
Oil tempera on cardboard
41.2 × 33.3 cm
Paula-Modersohn-Becker-Stiftung, Bremen, on loan from a private collection
Busch/Werner 23
Fig. p. 18

Self-Portrait with View from the Artist's Studio in Paris, 1900
Oil tempera on paper on cardboard
38 × 25.5 cm
Paula-Modersohn-Becker-Stiftung, Bremen, on loan from a private collection
Busch/Werner 49
Fig. p. 21

Moor Ditch, 1900
Oil tempera on cardboard
39.5 × 53 cm
Paula-Modersohn-Becker-Stiftung, Bremen
Busch/Werner 105
Fig. pp. 38/39

Moon over Landscape, c. 1900
Oil tempera on cardboard on hardboard
42 × 55.5 cm
Paula-Modersohn-Becker-Stiftung, Bremen
Busch/Werner 118
Fig. pp. 34/35

Children with Lanterns in front of a House, 1901
Oil tempera on cardboard
40.5 × 57.2 cm
Kunsthandel Wolfgang Werner, Bremen/Berlin
Busch/Werner 194
Fig. p. 31

Girl Sitting among Trees in a Meadow with Blooming Windflowers, c. 1901
Oil tempera on canvas
110 × 100 cm
Paula-Modersohn-Becker-Stiftung, Bremen, on loan from a private collection
Busch/Werner 198
Fig. p. 42

Elsbeth, c. 1902
Oil tempera on cardboard
32 × 28 cm
Paula-Modersohn-Becker-Stiftung, Bremen, on loan from a private collection
Busch/Werner 269
Fig. p. 32

Bust Portrait of a Farm Woman in a Red Dress, 1903
Oil tempera on cardboard on wood
40.5 × 37.8 cm
Paula-Modersohn-Becker-Stiftung, Bremen
Busch/Werner 372
Fig. p. 24

Seated Old Woman with Handkerchief, c. 1903
Oil tempera on cardboard
69.1 × 55.4 cm
Paula Modersohn-Becker Museum, Bremen
Busch/Werner 379
Fig. p. 25

Birch Trunk in front of a Landscape, c. 1903
Oil tempera on cardboard
59.4 × 47 cm
Paula Modersohn-Becker Museum, Bremen
Busch/Werner 446
Fig. p. 40

Seated Girl Nude with Her Legs Drawn Up I (Elsbeth), c. 1904
Oil tempera on cardboard on wood
68 × 57 cm
Paula-Modersohn-Becker-Stiftung, Bremen, on loan from a private collection
Busch/Werner 455
Fig. p. 79

Child on a Red-Patterned Cushion, c. 1904
Oil tempera on canvas
66.2 × 58 cm
Paula Modersohn-Becker Museum, Bremen
Busch/Werner 461
Fig. p. 43

Shooting Festival with Carousel II, 1904
Oil tempera on cardboard
56 × 73 cm
Paula Modersohn-Becker Museum, Bremen
Busch/Werner 526
Fig. p. 33

Self-Portrait with Red Rose, c. 1905
Oil tempera on cardboard on wood
66 × 46.5 cm
Paula-Modersohn-Becker-Stiftung, Bremen, on loan from a private collection
Busch/Werner 534
Fig. p. 49

The Sculptor Clara Rilke-Westhoff, 1905
Oil tempera on canvas
52 × 36.8 cm
Hamburger Kunsthalle
Busch/Werner 537
Fig. p. 48

Girl Playing the Flute in a Birch Forest, 1905
Oil tempera on canvas
110.4 × 90.2 cm
Paula Modersohn-Becker Museum, Bremen
Busch/Werner 602
Fig. p. 41

Still Life with Pumpkin and Ginger Pot, 1905
Oil tempera on canvas
75 × 95 cm
Von der Heydt-Museum, Wuppertal
Busch/Werner 622
Fig. p. 62

Still Life with Milk Bowl, 1905
Oil tempera on cardboard
55.2 × 71.8 cm
Paula Modersohn-Becker Museum, Bremen
Busch/Werner 623
Fig. p. 63

Self-Portrait on the 6th Wedding Anniversary, 1906
Oil tempera on cardboard on wood
101.8 × 70.2 cm
Paula Modersohn-Becker Museum, Bremen
Busch/Werner 628
Fig. p. 83

Self-Portrait as Standing Nude with Hat, 1906
Oil tempera on canvas
40 × 19.5 cm
Paula-Modersohn-Becker-Stiftung, Bremen, on loan from a private collection
Busch/Werner 629
Fig. p. 82

Large Standing Girl Nude, 1905/06
Oil tempera on canvas
135.6 × 50.8 cm
Paula Modersohn-Becker Museum, Bremen
Busch/Werner 632
Fig. p. 77

Standing Girl Nude with Hands Crossed, 1905/06
Charcoal on yellowish paper
40 × 22.8 cm
Paula Modersohn-Becker Museum, Bremen
Röver-Kann/Werner E V/10
Fig. p. 76

Seated Girl Nude with Apple, 1906
Oil tempera on canvas on wood
45.4 × 23.2 cm
Paula Modersohn-Becker Museum, Bremen
Busch/Werner 633
Fig. p. 80

Small Standing Girl Nude with Necklace and Rose, 1906
Oil tempera on canvas
35.3 × 28.5 cm
Paula Modersohn-Becker Museum, Bremen
Busch/Werner 634
Fig. p. 68

Portrait of Martha Vogeler in front of a Winter Landscape, 1906
Oil tempera on cardboard
54.7 × 48.3 cm
Private collection
Busch/Werner 636
Fig. p. 52

Portrait of Sister Herma with Artichoke Blossom in Raised Hand, 1906
Oil tempera on canvas
56.5 × 51 cm
Paula-Modersohn-Becker-Stiftung, Bremen, on loan from a private collection
Busch/Werner 640
Fig. p. 50

Portrait of Rainer Maria Rilke, 1906
Oil tempera on cardboard on wood
32.3 × 25.4 cm
Paula-Modersohn-Becker-Stiftung, Bremen, on loan from a private collection
Busch/Werner 643
Fig. p. 53

Seated Girl in White Shirt and Standing Girl Nude, May/June 1906
Oil tempera on cardboard on wood
95.9 × 63.6 cm
Paula Modersohn-Becker Museum, Bremen
Busch/Werner 651
Fig. p. 78

Seated Mother with Child in Her Lap, 1906
Oil tempera on cardboard
105.5 × 75 cm
Von der Heydt-Museum, Wuppertal
Busch/Werner 655
Fig. p. 81

Reclining Mother with Child II, summer, 1906
Oil tempera on canvas
82.5 × 124.7 cm
Paula Modersohn-Becker Museum, Bremen
Busch/Werner 657
Fig. pp. 70/71

Still Life with Clay Jug, Peonies and Oranges, 1906
Oil tempera on cardboard
61 × 49.5 cm
Kunsthandel Wolfgang Werner, Bremen/Berlin
Busch/Werner 669
Fig. p. 67

Self-Portrait Half-Turned to the Right, Her Hand on Her Chin, summer, 1906
Oil tempera on canvas
27 × 18.7 cm
Paula Modersohn-Becker Museum, Bremen, Purchased with the support of the Ernst von Siemens Kunststiftung, Kulturstiftung der Länder and a private donor
Busch/Werner 676
Fig. p. 58

Semi-Nude Self-Portrait with Amber Necklace II, 1906
Oil tempera on canvas
61 × 50 cm
Kunstmuseum Basel
Busch/Werner 679
Fig. p. 85

Self-Portrait with Lemon, 1906/07
Oil tempera on cardboard
50 × 27.5 cm
Paula-Modersohn-Becker-Stiftung, Bremen, on loan from a private collection
Busch/Werner 683
Fig. p. 55

Self-Portrait with Sprig of Camellias, 1906/07
Oil tempera on cardboard on wood
61.5 × 30.5 cm
Museum Folkwang, Essen
Busch/Werner 684
Fig. p. 54

Portrait of Lee Hoetger in front of a Floral Background, 1906
Oil tempera on canvas
92.4 × 73.5 cm
Paula Modersohn-Becker Museum, Bremen
Busch/Werner 685
Fig. p. 51

Bust Portrait of Lee Hoetger with Flower, August 1906
Oil tempera on canvas
55.3 × 33.2 cm
Paula Modersohn-Becker Museum, Bremen
Busch/Werner 687
Fig. p. 56

Otto Modersohn Sleeping, 1907
Oil tempera on canvas
39.7 × 46.3 cm
Paula-Modersohn-Becker-Stiftung, Bremen
Busch/Werner 689
Fig. p. 57

Nude Girl with Flower Vases, 1907
Oil tempera on canvas
89 × 109 cm
Von der Heydt-Museum, Wuppertal
Busch/Werner 699
Fig. p. 69

Elsbeth between Fire Lillies, 1907
Oil tempera on canvas
70.7 × 34 cm
Paula Modersohn-Becker Museum, Bremen, on loan from a private collection
Busch/Werner 718
Fig. p. 44

Old Poorhouse Woman in the Garden with Glass Ball and Poppies, 1907
Oil tempera on canvas
96.3 × 80.2 cm
Paula Modersohn-Becker Museum, Bremen
Busch/Werner 720
Fig. p. 59

Adoration of the Magi, 1907
Oil tempera on cardboard
35.8 × 48.3 cm
Paula Modersohn-Becker Museum, Bremen, on loan from a private collection
Busch/Werner 721
Fig. p. 65

Still Life with Blue Box, 1907
Oil tempera on canvas
27.3 × 35.7 cm
Paula-Modersohn-Becker-Stiftung, Bremen
Busch/Werner 732
Fig. p. 64

CLARA RILKE-WESTHOFF (1878–1954)

Portrait of the Painter Paula Modersohn-Becker, 1899
Plaster
46.5 × 42 × 36.5 cm
Base: 9 × 42 × 26 cm
Paula-Modersohn-Becker-Stiftung, Bremen
Fig. p. 1

COLOPHON AND PICTURE CREDITS

This book has been published on the occasion of the exhibition

Becoming Paula
London Berlin Worpswede Paris

Paula Modersohn-Becker Museum
Bremen
8 February – 13 September 2026
www.museen-boettcherstrasse.de

EXHIBITION

Concept: Frank Schmidt / Henrike Hans / Wolfgang Werner
Director: Frank Schmidt
Administration: Denise Eichler, Erna Meyerdierks
Research Associate: Henrike Hans
PR and Marketing: Cathrin Janke
Art Education: Anne Beel
Federal Volunteer Service: Sam Eisele
Shop: Maike Sotrop
Technical Management: Stefan Melzer
Conservation Care: Amelie Menck, Julia Tholen
Exhibition Graphics and Printed Materials: BrücknerAping. Büro für Gestaltung

CATALOGUE

Editor: Frank Schmidt for the Museen Böttcherstraße
Concept and Editing: Frank Schmidt
Project Management, Hirmer Verlag: Karen Angne, Verena Hüttner
Translation from the German: Gérard Goodrow, Cologne
Copy-Editing: Danko Szabó, Gräfelfing
Graphic Design and Typesetting: BrücknerAping. Büro für Gestaltung, Bremen
Production: Katja Durchholz
Prepress: SMS I Scheer Medien Service, Bremen
Paper: Munken Lynx naturweiß 170 g/m²
Typeface: GT Walsheim
Printing and Binding: Printer Trento S.p.A., Trento

Printed in Italy

Bibliographic information published by the Deutsche Nationalbibliothek
The Deutsche Nationalbibliothek lists this publication in the Deutsche Nationalbibliografie; detailed bibliographic data is available on the Internet at https://www.dnb.de.

ISBN 978-3-7774-4782-7 (English trade edition)
ISBN 978-3-7774-4776-6 (German trade edition)

Hirmer Publishers
(Hirmer Verlag GmbH)
Managing Director: Kerstin Ludolph
Bayerstraße 57–59
80335 Munich
Germany

www.hirmerpublishers.com
www.hirmerpublishers.co.uk

Cover Image:
Self-Portrait with Lemon, 1906/07 (detail), Paula-Modersohn-Becker-Stiftung, Bremen, on loan from a private collection

Picture Credits:
© Paula Modersohn-Becker Museum, Bremen, figs. pp. 25, 33, 40, 41, 43, 44, 51, 56, 58, 59, 63, 65, 68, 70/71, 72, 76, 77, 78, 80, 83
© Paula-Modersohn-Becker-Stiftung, Bremen, figs. pp. 8/9, 11–24, 26–32, 34–39, 42, 45–50, 52–55, 57, 60/61, 62, 64, 67, 69, 73–75, 79, 81, 82, 84–90

PAULA MODERSOHN-BECKER MUSEUM

Museen Böttcherstraße Stiftungs-GmbH
Paula Modersohn-Becker Museum
Böttcherstr. 6, 28195 Bremen
T +49 421 33882 22
info@museen-boettcherstrasse.de
www.museen-boettcherstrasse.de

Die Sparkasse Bremen
KARIN UND UWE HOLLWEG STIFTUNG
MIX Paper | Supporting responsible forestry FSC® C015829
Die Arbeitgeber. DIE UNTERNEHMENSVERBÄNDE IM LANDE BREMEN E.V.
Bremer Landesbank Stiftung